D1070874

WORLD TECHNOLOGY & HUMAN DESTINY

world technology and human destiny

EDITED BY RAYMOND ARON

Ann Arbor: The University of Michigan Press

Copyright © by The University of Michigan 1963
All rights reserved
Originally *Colloques de Rheinfelden,* copyright Calmann-Lévy 1960
Library of Congress Catalog Card No. 62-18444
Translated by Richard Seaver
Published in the United States of America by
The University of Michigan Press and simultaneously
in Toronto, Canada, by Ambassador Books Limited
Manufactured in the United States of America
by Vail-Ballou Press, Inc., Binghamton, N.Y.

301.24
W927

PREFACE

Raymond Aron conceived, prepared, and directed the Basel-Rheinfelden conference. The need for it had become increasingly clear in the course of the preceding conferences organized under the presidency of Michael Polanyi. The over-all title given them was "Tradition and Evolution."

The technical revolution is spreading throughout the world; new techniques are revolutionizing our way of life. But does the industrial society dictate to the mind—to the point of imposing a determined ideology upon it—or do our moral values allow us to impress various forms on this society?

Necessity and liberty, the one and the many, instrumental values and ultimate values present questions of a philosophical nature that Raymond Aron felt should be discussed by philosophers, but not in an abstract way. The originality of the Basel-Rheinfelden conference lies in the fact that eminent theoreticians and specialists have been called upon to make concrete predictions and give their opinions on a wide range of subjects.

It was practically impossible to include within the limits of a single volume the richness of the Rheinfelden conversations. In any event, much had to be condensed, therefore much sacrificed. But the cutting was also extremely uneven. As was to be expected, the discussions grew animated and strayed far from the main subject, and, although these were often the most interesting and fruitful exchanges, they had to be eliminated for the sake of unity.

v

UNIVERSITY LIBRARIES
CARNEGIE MELLON UNIVERSITY
PITTSBURGH, PA   15213-3890

Throughout the conference, Raymond Aron tried constantly to keep the discussion from straying too far afield; the two university students, Jean-Claude Casanova and Pierre Hassner, to whom the job of preparing the present volume was entrusted, followed Mr. Aron's example. They sincerely regret that their concern for unity necessitated the elimination of certain remarks and the condensation of others which they, as observers, found particularly striking. They hope the participants will forgive them the methods used to focus the discussions on the main themes.

The Congress for the Liberty of Culture warmly thanks all the participants who contributed their various talents to the conference and made it such a resounding success.

J.-C. C. and P. H.

CONTENTS

Reports

INDUSTRIAL SOCIETY AND THE POLITICAL DIALOGUES OF THE WEST

BY RAYMOND ARON

Are we living in an age of ideological schism comparable to the wars of religion? Or, rather, have the same ideals spread throughout the world and have the controversies, in spite of their violence, to do with means rather than ends, techniques rather than values? An observer, at times impressed by the similarity of vocabulary employed by the communists and the West and sometimes struck by the impossibility of any real exchange between them, hesitates between the two opposing viewpoints.

In the established democracies, parties seem hard pressed to find areas of basic disagreement. Philosophers, although agreeing on the ends, are incapable of formulating in terms acceptable to everyone the objectives of which almost everyone approves. Western man knows what he wants better than his reasons for wanting it.

Seen from the West, the situation in the communist countries seems exactly the opposite. Should the society which socialist countries are building be essentially different from that which the West deems good? Is communism merely a method for overtaking more quickly the level of productivity already attained by the United States? Or is this level of productivity itself only a means toward the end of a communist society? If so, how does this society differ from a so-called democratic society?

On both sides of the Iron Curtain men disagree concerning the answers to these questions. Although officially every com-

3

munist is bound to proclaim the essential difference between the two regimes, there are Soviet citizens who privately admit to the thesis of basic similarity, just as there are Westerners who believe in the essential difference (although their reasons are of course different from those of communists who reach the same conclusion).

In the underdeveloped countries some people become communists because they see in communism the most rapid and efficacious path to industrialization, while others believe it offers the ideal of a good society.

Each of the three worlds—the West, the Soviet, and the underdeveloped countries—is examining the nature of its own society and its relationship to the others.

I. *The Technical-Ideological Debate*

If we compare the political discussions of the 1930's and those of the 1950's in the established democracies, we cannot help but be struck by the contrast. Fascism and communism have virtually disappeared as respectable doctrines and there is an area of common accord between the parties—the parliamentary socialists and enlightened conservatives, for example—who respect the rules of the game. The areas of disagreement are of secondary importance, although this applies more to Sweden than to Great Britain. The fact itself is not open to discussion: what we still have to determine is how to interpret this "fact"; or, to put it more precisely, whether the 1950's can tell us more about the society in which we live than the 1930's.

Speaking for myself—and this will be the initial premise of this paper—I am sure that the 1950's are more characteristic of the industrial society than were the 1930's. Whatever the future may hold, certain results can be considered as already established.

1. The status of property, in a Western-type economic and political regime, is no longer considered decisive, even by parties of Marxist tendencies. There are many reasons for the ideological "devaluation" of the traditional theme of nationalizing the

instruments of production. We shall do no more than list them: the similarity between public and private enterprise in the areas of technical and administrative organization, working conditions, and rates of pay; the prevailing concern with productivity, with nationalization offering no absolute guarantee of efficiency; the continuing drawbacks of abnormally large or monopolistic organizations, even when the property of industrial concentrations has been collectivized; the advantages of a number of management centers and the necessity of reconstituting relatively autonomous enterprises, even assuming generalized nationalization and total planning. Nor is it certain that, within the framework of a democratic state, the directors of public enterprises exert any less pressure on the political leaders than do the directors, owners, or managers of private businesses.

2. The thesis of capitalist anarchy and capitalist contradictions has been ideologically discredited because all regulatory methods are imperfect and the imperfections of total planning appear to be no less serious than those of partial planning or market mechanisms. The economic crisis of the 1930's seemed to confirm the Marxist theories. Private property and competition did seem to produce a regime which was not viable. The theory of "maturity" was fashionable. Keynes cited the disappearance or reduction of the number of profitable capital investments. The reformers of capitalism were half socialist, or even Marxist. Twenty years later the advocates of maturity seem in turn outmoded. All the countries of Western Europe, measuring themselves against the United States, realize how far they still have to go along the path of industrial development. They are no longer afraid of the lack of opportunity for profitable investment, but rather of an insufficiency of uninvested capital.

Even in the United States, economic growth in intensity seems unlimited, not by the conquest of new territories or the subjugation of peoples, not by bringing the underdeveloped countries into the capitalist orbit, but by increased productivity and the discovery of new goods to manufacture and new methods to make them.

3. In this expanding economy, the problem of distribution takes on a radically different meaning from that it has always had through the ages. General wealth was thought of as an almost constant quantity, determined once and for all: if one person had too much of it, another had too little. But as soon as collective wealth increases by x per cent a year, the attraction of growth becomes more important, even for the underprivileged, than any plan for redistribution.

Economists have been saying for a long time that the size of the cake is more important than the way it is cut. They knew that everyone's share increased as the size of the cake increased. But as long as the economists had their eyes fixed on ephemeral fluctuations and were worried about "maturity," growth did not seem to be the major factor. Recent trends throughout the Western world have, however, confirmed the fact that the distribution of income tends to be less unequal as the collective wealth increases. The combination of a capitalist economy and a representative regime gives the people's elected representatives an ever increasing influence. Governments are able to "redistribute incomes," especially by direct taxation, and in various ways to modify for the benefit of the less privileged the division of income which would have resulted spontaneously from the market mechanisms.

Private property versus public ownership, anarchy of the market versus planned economy, capitalist exploitation versus equality—the three themes of socialist doctrine—have lost a great deal of their force. Whether the issue is the status of property, planning, or the equalization of income, henceforth it is not so much a question of choosing between two alternatives than of combining two complementary methods, of deciding how far one should go in a given direction.

One might object that what happened in the 1930's might recur tomorrow. Any prolonged and serious economic crisis would endanger the political regime; that is an uncontested fact. But unless a government were exceptionally incompetent it seems highly improbable to us that a depression comparable to that of the 1930's could happen again. Public opinion would not tolerate it, the experts are convinced they have the means to prevent it, and governments would be compelled to take steps to end it. There is no longer any question of accepting economic crises as inevitable natural phenomena which are part and parcel of human destiny. The rejection of economic fatalism, which is now an integral part of the political conscience of the West, insures us that the authorities will intervene to mitigate any temporary fluctuation of the economy.

There is nothing terribly original about this way of thinking. Not all of the major doctrines formulated at the beginning of the nineteenth century considered that the conflict between capitalism and socialism was final. According to the philosophy of Auguste Comte, human beings affect the workings of industrial society, and this society has certain characteristic traits which are not dependent on the outcome of the struggle between workers and capitalists. Auguste Comte did not believe that the class struggle was fruitful, nor did he believe that the nationalization of the instruments of production was a virtue. For him the problem was twofold: to organize industrial society in a rational way on the temporal level of efficiency or work, and to subordinate the powerful and the wealthy to spiritual authority.

A social-economic theory centered around the fact of growth and the consequences which it entails, freed from the radical alternatives bequeathed by Marxist heritage (public ownership—private property, planning—market, equality—exploitation), is in itself no assurance of social harmony. A democratic society in a state of growth is subject to multiple debates which I call technical-ideological because the attitudes adopted by this or that advocate depend (in varying degrees) on technical considerations and ethical or doctrinal arguments.

At the lowest level, the controversy continually revolves around the equitable distribution of sacrifices and rewards between individuals and classes. Given that every citizen desires the greatest possible growth of the economy, there would still be room for discussion among the spokesmen for various social groups concerning the division of income (to the extent that this division is influenced by the public authorities).

Actually, the problem is never that simple. Almost invariably three problems which are logically distinct from one another are raised simultaneously: How best to stimulate growth? How to distribute income fairly? How to insure the internal or external equilibrium of the economy, both the relative stability of prices and the equilibrium in the balance of payments? A policy aimed at reducing inequality is not necessarily in conflict with the necessities of expansion (Sweden, for example). A sound currency policy is not inherently opposed to growth (West Germany). But it sometimes happens that the requirements of sound currency can paralyze expansion (as was the case with Great Britain from 1956–58). And it can happen that the struggle against inflation may turn into a struggle against the power of the unions. Each party tries to resolve the technical problem according to its own theoretical conceptions and by methods it deems its voters will approve.

Since the war, this is how parties have operated and formulated their programs. In France, the so-called parties of the left have tended to be expansionist and inflationist; in the United States they are more "extravagant"; in Great Britain more given to "physical controls." The so-called parties of the right have everywhere been concerned with solidifying and strengthening their currencies; in the United States they are more "economy minded" and rigid; in Great Britain they rely heavily on monetary techniques; in West Germany they are staunch advocates of market mechanisms. Do these positions correspond to the real interests of the social groups represented by the various parties or are they the residue of outdated theories? In any case, the success of the methods of the right is better for the masses than the failure of the methods of the left. This explains the relative political apathy of the masses in an industrial society: an effective government of the right will be legitimately popular, even with the voters of the left or extreme left, while

an ineffective government of the left will be deservedly un-
popular.

Above these current controversies, political theorists of every
leaning try to formulate philosophies for their parties and their
programs. But in the established democracies all parties agree
as to the method of democratic government (representative,
parliamentary, or presidential); the mixed, expansionist economy with social legislation and redistribution of income; the
renunciation of colonial domination. About what then, from the
point of view of doctrine, do they disagree?

It seems to me that the themes are the following: First, the
question of equality, or, to be more exact, how much emphasis
to place on the various forms of inequality. To what extent is
it desirable—or possible—to reduce the inequalities of income?
To what extent is it desirable—or possible—to eliminate the in-
heritance of wealth in order to limit economic inequalities to a
lifetime and make them inseparable from the merits of the individual? To what extent is it desirable—or possible—to make
sure that everyone has an equal start in life in order to increase
social mobility (democratic reform of education)?

A second point of doctrinal conflict is that of liberty. But
since theorists basically agree about political institutions, the
debate has been transferred to another plane. Since political
institutions guarantee formal liberties, we study the relationship between the freedom of the individual and mass organizations (such as unions), or collective managements, or the state
itself. The theme of freedom versus the new despotism belongs
to the new liberalism and the new right rather than to the new
left.

These themes are part of the secular tradition of political
thought. What is new is the extension of the area of agreement
between the parties and the awareness of the necessities of industrial civilization. Only the margin of freedom allowed by that
civilization is open to reasonable discussion. Controversy is
also possible on metaphysical or religious issues. Materialists

and Catholics of good will can arrive at a seemingly analogous social action, but the deeper meaning they impart to it is completely different, as is the meaning they give their existence.

Between the limited differences of the constitutional parties and the radical differences based on metaphysical or religious concepts there are the ideological differences which flare up when conceptions of social organization are, or seem to be, completely irreconcilable; when these conceptions spring from conflicting viewpoints; or when arguments about the form of property or control develop into a clash over essentials (or when in the heat of the moment they are made to seem irreconcilable, which comes to the same thing). This is what happens in democratic countries where, through a revolt against reality, through misunderstanding, or through faith, there is a strong Communist party.

The democratic socialist is among those who want to develop an industrial society within the political framework of free discussion. The communist demands complete power for himself and exclusive adherence to his ideology. And when impassioned debate for or against a party with monopolistic pretentions enters the arena of reasonable discussion among constitutional parties, we have the feeling of living in an age of schism. But when the totalitarian parties disappear, we have the opposite impression of sinking into a period of middle-class comfort and prosaic ratiocination, unless of course circumstances arise in which the status of the community itself is jeopardized on an international level. In Great Britain, although anticolonialism is standard doctrine, the Suez expedition aroused a hornet's nest of reaction. In France, where anticolonialism has never been accepted doctrine, the Algerian situation also provoked bitter controversy. The situation in France is complex and contradictory because the progress of industrial civilization is rendering old controversies obsolete while at the same time the crisis of the French empire and the persistence of the Communist party are keeping ancient passions alive.

II. *The West and the Soviet Reality*

In the established democracies, industrial society allows for current discussion concerning the management of business and doctrinal research. The former has to do with the priority to be given various goals (expansion, equality, equilibrium, freedom of the unions) approved by everyone. The latter tries to bring institutions into line with traditional preferences (conservatism, liberalism, socialism) and keep them compatible with the structure of industrial society. But, whether established or not, the Western democracies are confronted with a society which derives from an ideology—the Soviet Union. Even in countries where communism is practically nonexistent, such as the United States, the Soviet Union looms as an ideological menace. There is no political philosophy in the West which is not shaped by the interpretation it gives the facts of communism and the Soviet reality.

The Soviet system is characterized by several economic and social traits: rapid industrialization, an emphasis on heavy rather than light industry and on investment rather than consumption, development of services and substructure at a lower level than in the Western societies at a similar phase of their development, rigid planning made possible by the nationalization of all businesses, etc. What is more, there is only one political party in the Soviet Union; its ideology is that of the society as well as the state, and all members of the ruling class belong to it. The absence of competition among parties for the exercise of power, the ban on any discussion of official doctrine and even on the decisions which the authorities convert into official doctrine, make for a type of political regime which is basically opposed to that of the Western democracies. What is the historical and philosophical meaning of this opposition?

The job of the economist is to determine what these different economic systems have in common and how they differ. Urbanization, industrialization, the lowering of consumption in the initial stages of industrialization, organization of businesses according to the law of output, diversion of a portion of the total population's annual resources for investment purposes: these are all phenomena which occur in any kind of industrial society. On the other hand, the allocation of resources for various uses is made differently and various organs (banks, ministries, interest rates) serve different purposes on either side of the Iron Curtain.

Economists are still discussing the tendencies of the Soviet system's evolution. To what extent, from the standpoint of economics, does the Soviet regime tend to move closer to the Western model? Won't investment decisions require more and more rigorous calculations as the possibilities multiply and the choices become more difficult? Unless communism actually applies the theory of pauperization—which Marx predicted for capitalism —the standard of living is bound to rise on the other side of the Iron Curtain. And will not an increase in wealth lead necessarily to middle-class ideas and habits?

If this is true, then the Soviet system would be merely a substitute for capitalism in the initial stages of industrialization. Even so, the Soviet fact would pose two serious problems: How long will Soviet governments subordinate welfare to power and make their primary objective the economic-military strength of the collective whole? If the Soviet technique for industrialization is effective at a certain stage of development, does the philosopher have to condone—for the sake of the future—the necessity for methods he knows are inhuman? We will come back to this last problem later on. As for the first, its significance is both immediate (what are Soviet intentions vis-à-vis the rest of the world?) and enduring (what will men do with the limitless means that science puts in their hands?).

But this rational explanation of the Soviet regime is open to dispute. Western socialists, especially those of the left, wanting to reconcile their preference for planning with their political liberalism, like to think that as soon as the period of intensive capital accumulation is past the Soviet economy will move closer to Western methods and as a result the political regime will be transformed. We are not concerned here with either defending or rejecting this interpretation, but it is highly relevant to the question at hand: is the goal of the Soviet regime, as its doctrine suggests, the welfare of the individual, and have its industrial techniques been instituted to attain that goal more quickly? Is totalitarianism therefore merely a by-product of this excessive speed?

This effort to rationalize Stalinist totalitarianism is not confined to the West. Some Soviet intellectuals also virtually subscribe to it in private. The close affinity of both regimes as to their economies and their economic goals is suggested by the language used by both sides: "Catch up to and pass the United States in productivity." Thus economic growth is the common cause of all countries, with the West in the lead but the others presently closing the gap.

Soviet spokesmen may claim that their rate of growth is faster than that of the West. Even so, it is a question of the relative advantage of a regime which is not fundamentally different from its rivals. And besides, what is the price paid for this advantage? Is the regime's progress faster because it assures a higher output of work per capita or because it imposes greater sacrifices on its people? And there are other characteristics of the Soviet system which its advocates or detractors could cite to excuse or defend the Soviet economy (or the economy of the West): greater freedom of action for those in charge of planning, fewer guarantees for the individual, concentration of capital, greater risk of serious error, difficulties of economic calculation, etc.

But the fundamental question is: do the communists want to build an industrial society of the same kind as that of the West? A single-party system, obsessive propaganda, police terror: are all these phenomena the temporary adjunct of an ambitious and precipitant program, the indispensable means for an unprecedented collective effort? Or, on the contrary, have industry, capital investment, and ideology become the instruments of a system bent on total domination? Is the aim of communism, as it has been established in Russia, to reach by another route the high standard of living and personal freedom of the West? Or is it to establish, in the guise of affluence and liberation, a system of absolute tyranny? The interpetation of the present historical moment depends largely on how one answers these questions.

While we do not intend to offer a detailed reply to this crucial question, the two extreme positions are well known. On the one hand there is that of Mr. Isaac Deutscher whose adherents we shall call neo-Marxists, and on the other that of Mrs. Hanna Arendt. Other intermediate positions are easy enough to think of, and I shall offer one of my own that lies between the two extremes.

To reduce totalitarianism to the means or the adjunct of industrial society is to misunderstand certain historical facts. The rejection of a plurality of parties and ideologies predates the five-year plans and is part and parcel of the very essence of Bolshevism, which from its inception decreed itself one with the proletariat and considered all others either enemies or traitors. The example of National Socialism proves that the rejection of reasonable debate can occur in any society at any stage of its economic development. But neo-Marxism, whose optimism is based on an extreme rationalism, makes two other mistakes. A means can be transformed into an end, especially if the means was the result of a contradiction. Marxism, which proclaimed a predetermined order of succession from one regime to the next, has been used to justify a regime which was fulfilling the functions of the very regime it was supposed to succeed (thus explaining the contradiction between the two slogans: "Catching up to the United States" and "Socialism is the heir of capitalism"). Bolshevism has never been able to extricate itself from this initial and fundamental lie, and when, after the Twentieth Party Congress, Poland and Hungary did try to discard it, the collapse soon followed. It is in fact impossible for communism to be presented in the guise offered by the Soviets without its losing prestige and its utopian significance.

Reducing it to the slogan of "catching up to the United States," or merely doing differently, or better, or later what capitalism has already done, does not suffice to lend communism the prestige of the future or of an absolute value. Thus the Bolsheviks were led to claim as essential merits those very characteristics of their doctrine and system which the neo-Marxists and Western liberals consider as the price paid for rapid industrialization, that is, ideological totalitarianism, identification of the party and the proletariat, the rejection of competing political parties. The banning of open discussion and the claim to infallibility have become inseparable from communism, which began to loom as some strange form of pseudo-religious fanaticism, foundering in irrationality yet constantly invoking reason, always straining to convert or enslave heretics.

The second mistake of the neo-Marxists is to subscribe unconsciously to a naive idea of human unity. Neither science nor the technical applications which every society wants to utilize implies that one social organization, and only one, is bound to spread throughout the world. The originality of Western societies has been its several classes, its distinction between temporal and spiritual power, and the acceptance of a certain competition among the various community groups. This Western originality can survive in the industrial age, but that is no proof that it must spread wherever its techniques are used. The Asiatic mode of production, to recall Marx's concept recently utilized by Professor Wittfogel, is liable to continue for a long time, but sustained and renewed by modern methods. In other terms, an industrial society can be monolithic and not pluralistic, divided into a passive mass and a single hierarchy, bureaucratic and statist, with a minimum of discussion between schools of thought and a minimum of competition between autonomous organizations. Whatever similarities there may be between the economies, the methods of production, and the machines, it is likely that the conflict between pluralistic societies (several classes and ideologies) and the monist society will continue, the former differentiating between society and state and the latter identifying the two.

In the West, polemics against Stalinism are no longer a subject of philosophical interest. After Khrushchev's speech at the Twentieth Party Congress there is no longer any need to show that Stalin was a bloody tyrant. But discussion is still raging among sociologists concerning the economic, social, and political make-up of the Soviet regime as compared to those of the West, both in the past and in the future. And it is still raging as to the intrinsic meaning and goal of the communist venture, its power or ideas. Does it aim at the establishment of an industrial society whose values would be comparable to those of the West, or rather at the utilization of modern methods and techniques in the service of the original impulse toward violence and domination, an impulse inherent in man's nature but which, with the weapons of massive destruction now available, would confront humanity with the choice of total submission or total annihilation.

III.   *The West, the "Third World," and Atomic Weapons*

The Soviet system is an answer of a half-Western people to the industrial civilization which began in the West. The way in which the West and the Soviets themselves interpret this answer largely determines the meaning to be given two other problems which confront the West: the bomb and the under-developed countries.

Both these problems are the consequence and, so to speak, the expression of the civilization in which we live. Both are a result of the prodigious increase in our ability to produce and our even greater ability to destroy; of the complete rationalization of certain activities, the nonrationalization of others, and the impossibility of a complete rationalization.

At first glance, it seems accidental that the atomic and thermo-nuclear bombs should have been perfected at the same time as the conflict between the Soviet and Western regimes, and to a certain extent it is. But there are deep-rooted causes for each. Sooner or later, man, with his constantly increasing knowledge, was bound to acquire the capacity to manipulate natural forces to the point of completely controlling his own destiny. At the end of the road opened by the Promethean act lay the capacity of autodestruction. Every individual has always been able to kill himself and to kill his fellow man; now the most powerful societies have the means to render the planet uninhabitable.

Thus humanity is faced with three possibilities: apocalyptic war, which would put an end to civilization as we know it and even to humanity itself; the continuation of traditional politics while avoiding total war (in other words, continuation of the diplomacy of the past ten years); or, finally, a fundamental historical change whereby individuals and societies are won over to any international policy which would exclude war. Which of the three paths humanity will take depends in part on the meaning of the conflict between East and West.

If Soviet society is totalitarian merely by accident—because it is passing through a pre-industrialization phase and wants to close the gap—the crisis caused by the discovery of the ultimate weapon right after World War II is only ephemeral. For a long time the unequitable development of various societies was inevitable: if the Soviet Union is totalitarian basically because it is a relatively underdeveloped country, then it will soon cease to be totalitarian and the dangers of the ultimate weapon will no longer be multiplied by the intense hostility between the Soviet and Western worlds. If, on the other hand, the goal of Soviet society is radically different from that of the West (concentration of mass power, unification of state and society), even more if totalitarianism is the expression of a temptation from which no individual or society is free, then the coincidence of the ultimate weapon and the serious schism between the Soviet and Western worlds—no matter how the present crisis may resolve itself—reveals the existentialist situation which mankind must face squarely: the desire for absolute power threatens to condemn those societies which possess weapons of massive destructive power with mass suicide.

The "third world," * as the West sees it, is also the result of industrial society and of the Soviet-Western conflict. However one may define underdevelopment, it stems more than anything else from a disproportion between the growth in population and the growth of agricultural or industrial resources. This disproportion is itself the result of partial rationalization, or the unequal results of various processes of rationalization. There have been extraordinary advances in medicine and hygiene: to eliminate germs, contagious diseases, and epidemics costs only in the millions, or at the most hundreds of millions, of dollars. Compared to the bomb, the destructive techniques applied to insects and germs are both cheap and efficient, although medicine is far from having achieved the same degree of efficiency in combating diseases which affect life itself (cancer, leukemia). Above all, the population of the third world has not yet learned to apply rational birth control methods, and it is a much longer and costlier process to introduce rational work methods than it is to hand out antibiotics and DDT. Mastering matter is simpler than mastering life, destruction is easier than construction, and it is not nearly so difficult to expand the use of instruments and machines as it is to change men. For the first time in history the size of the world's population is no longer *naturally* limited by the world's resources. It is possible to bring children into the world for whom human conditions of existence cannot be provided. (Anyone who has been through Calcutta can vouch for this.) For this reason alone the third world confronts the philosophers of the West with many questions, some of which have received too much attention, while others have been practically ignored.

The first and most often discussed question is that of the revolt against colonialism and the resentment of the (relative) wealth of the West. European domination of a large part of Asia and Africa is in the process of disappearing, although the French and English are trying to maintain their sovereignty or to create

* The underdeveloped countries of the world that are unaligned with the East or the West.

interracial communities wherever there is an important European minority (Algeria, Kenya, Rhodesia). What is the best way to withdraw? Has this withdrawal been too fast or not fast enough? What is its effect on the living conditions of native populations? Hasn't the withdrawal sometimes become a form of European self-seeking? (Colonies are no longer profitable businesses, costing more than they bring in, since to make them viable requires considerable capital investment.) One ethnologist coined the phrase: "Anti-colonialism, the alibi of pauperization." The philosopher does not have to join the debate. For better or worse, it is fairly obvious that anticolonialism has got the upper hand. And even if France succeeds in establishing a Negro African community, or if England manages to set up interracial states in East Africa, the majority of the ex-colonial peoples will still have to work out their own salvation and shape their own destinies as sovereign states in an industrial age. Just what the West can and must do to help these peoples who have emerged from the colonial period suffering from overpopulation and poverty is in each case a matter for the economists, sociologists, and politicians to determine. There is no need for philosophers to ponder this problem. Having recognized the right of people to work out their own destiny, and realizing that the job of the conquerors is, to quote Montesquieu, one of repairing the evils of conquest, the liquidation of colonial situations creates inconsistencies of the same sort as those that result from the plurality of objectives in a situation of economic expansion. In the case of poverty-ridden populations who lack both technicians and equipment, the yearning for independence cannot be satisfied without disappointing the desire for better living conditions.

An even more serious problem is the moral contradiction which, compared with the West, results from the dual necessity of wanting both material development and a good society. If only totalitarian techniques, more or less modeled after Russian communism, suffice to end the vicious cycle of poverty and achieve the initial stages of industrialization, what can the West say? That there is no proof that totalitarian techniques are indispensable or the only practical method of development? Granted that the proof has never been given, but at least the case is conceivable and raises a philosophical problem. It may again be objected that there is nothing essentially new in the discovery of the possible contradiction between efficiency and morality. And yet I think that there is something novel in the hypothesis that a regime might exist which, to our eyes, is necessary and at the same time fundamentally evil (compared to our own concept of what constitutes a good society and way of life). Why was such a hypothesis impossible in the past and why is there no record of it in classical political philosophy? Because a good regime normally seemed good both for the body and soul of a society, a regime in which laws were respected and people lived without fear, a regime which fostered the development of the population and commerce. In our time the size of the population is not governed by an automatic mechanism, since men no longer die of hunger. Throughout a large part of the world there are more people than there are resources, and the relation between the two obviously becomes a matter of top priority for the authorities. To put the liberty of the few above the equilibrium between population and resources implies a contempt of the masses and the abandoning of millions to misery, suggests that the needs of the many are subordinated to the adornments or excesses of the few, and ignores the need for total sacrifice toward the end of economic development. In most underdeveloped societies, material development signifies and implies social change and historical revolution. How can this revolution be accomplished without resorting to extreme measures of constraint? Some socialists who in their own country are liberal, come to the conclusion after some hesitation that communism is the answer in the underdeveloped countries. But how long will this totalitarian technique have to remain in force? And is it necessary that a concern for mankind involves subjecting it to tyranny and a system of lies? Never before our time has the potential antinomy between means and end been presented in such a way as it is today because of the necessity for economic development in countries where neither collective technique nor individual reason control the growth of the population.

Beyond this contradiction of material development there is another problem which is almost never raised: apart from science and its applied techniques, what are the other features of Western society that non-Westerners ought to, or would like to, adopt? To be specific, is the choice between Western democracy and the Soviet one-party system of universal importance or is it not? Most of the traditional regimes have, through Western influence, disappeared, but parliamentary methods have seldom taken root. The West cannot fail to want democracy to spread if we take democracy—aside from certain specific institutions —to mean a system under which the people govern themselves, have confidence in each other, and mutually assume that reason will prevail. But competition between parties and the procedures of representative institutions are specific historical phenomena and perhaps inseparable from certain traditions. Even in Western Europe it is obvious that the parliamentary system works less smoothly in Latin and Catholic countries than in Protestant countries or countries with a long tradition of communal liberties.

Isn't it time for the West to ask itself not only whether the political system it prefers is compatible with such and such a stage of industrialization but also whether this system is compatible with the customs and ideals of other civilizations? Under what circumstances can Western democracy succeed? Which aspects of this democracy can be considered as characteristic of a specific people and which are inseparable from the essence of industrial society and Western morality?

IV. *The Search for Reason*

No matter which of the three preceding dialogues we refer to, it seems clear that Western man is not living in an age of metaphysical or religious schisms. According to the optimists, the communist system is merely a shortcut to a society which does not differ essentially from that of the West, while to the pessimists it is the application of unprecedented means to the age-old objectives of power and coercion.

In the peaceful democracies of the West, the most impassioned debates have been occasioned by the conduct of foreign policy. It was the Suez expedition which split the English nation in two, not the nationalization of public services. It was the war in Algeria which brought France to the brink of civil war. The power of a nation and its rank in the world arouse more indignation and devotion than do the standard of living and the distribution of wealth.

It is easy enough for the West to understand the attraction of totalitarianism if, in the final analysis, it is merely the modern form of the impulse to violence and domination, the technique which makes total domination possible. Such an interpretation of totalitarianism would open tragic perspectives to humanity without offering anything new to the age-old debate of the philosophers. If, in the age of thermonuclear bombs, societies and their governments are not reasonable, an apocalyptic catastrophe could result.

As for the third world, it raises two new problems—new at least on this scale. From the moment science upset the natural mechanism by which the size of societies was regulated, the primary task of rulers was to impose a certain equilibrium between population and resources. Governments which fulfill this natural function do not merely employ methods which in themselves are deplorable, they also create (or may create) living conditions which the philosopher deems bad (inhuman) but which he does not necessarily condemn so long as he cannot discover any other technique for regulating the population-resources equilibrium.

On the other hand, science and the techniques of production now belong to all mankind. In certain respects, economic activity has become detached from its social context. As production methods spread throughout the world, what institutions will they take with them? Do non-Westerners want to, or are they compelled to, adopt certain elements of Western civilization such as a parliamentary system, political parties, a free press, and universities?

Whatever answer we give these questions, however we interpret these three dialogues—the West with itself, the West with the Soviet, and both with the third world—the West would appear, if this analysis were exhaustive, in the basic image of the "peaceful democracies," confronted by the reaction to its victories and defeats, by Russia's answer and the answer of former colonies subjected to Europe's transitory hegemony. And yet, as I see it, this is not the true situation. The three controversies which we have briefly examined are governed by a controversy within the West itself concerning the meaning of the industrial —or technical—society which is on the way to becoming the universal society.

Some indication of this fundamental debate was already evident in what I called the technical-ideological controversy. The real conservative is not the minister of finances who prefers monetary methods to administrative action in matters of goods or prices, nor is it the person who prefers the privately owned Citroën or General Motors to the nationalized Renault or Gorki factories. The conservative would like to preserve certain ways of life which he deems are good in themselves: hierarchies, property as a means of income, religious beliefs. In the same way, the liberal—in the European, not the American sense of the term—is not primarily interested in market mechanisms.

Conservatives and liberals alike, if we judge them by what they write and say, are upset about certain features of past societies and find fault with certain aspects of contemporary society. At the root of these regrets and criticisms lies the problem which obsessed philosophers at the beginning of the nineteenth century and which today we sometimes seem to have forgotten. What is the meaning, what is the nature of the society being shaped by science and industry? Or, to put it another way, what constitutes, for the past as well as the present, the "good life"? We do not produce for the sake of production, but in order to consume. But the purpose of life is not to consume, for in the case of basic needs (food, clothing, and shelter) satiety soon sets in, as it does, though less rapidly, for secondary needs (industrial products). An exception can be made for those people for whom secondary needs are a question of prestige or status, since snobbery is by definition insatiable. Are we then to conclude that leisure is the goal and the mechanization of production the means of freeing man from servile labor? If so, we are still faced with the same problem: what to do with the leisure which has become the goal in life? Power politics is out of date, since in the thermonuclear age the rivalries of national pride or power would lead to the suicide of humanity itself. The politics of industrial society, which we have hypothetically made universal, would be merely a matter of the rational and/or reasonable management of the production and distribution of goods. In this hypothetical world, would private life, recreation, and art have any meaningful place?

Raising questions about the industrial society should not be confused with the criticism of "mass culture" so frequently made in the United States. Criticism of mass culture can go so far as to question a society whose main objective seems to be that of achieving the maximum capacity to manipulate natural forces. Most often, this criticism, in which ex-Marxists and conservatives particularly delight, does no more than point out and deplore (for specific reasons) the mediocrity of mass culture in affluent societies. To transcend this stage, it is necessary to recognize the validity, or rather the necessity, of philosophical interrogation. And yet in this century, an age in which, to use the well-known phrase, politics is fate, there is no agreement as to either the method or goal of political philosophy.

In certain countries such as Great Britain, political philosophy is a kind of speculation which was practiced in past centuries and is now a matter of historical interest. The influence of logical positivism combines with a large degree of unanimity on basic issues (mixed economy, parliamentary regime) to discourage a truly philosophical study of the problems of social organization. Elsewhere, in France for example, there has been no dearth of impassioned political-ideological discussion during the postwar years, but it has been extremely confused because France's own problems (loss of national prestige, slow industrialization) have been mixed in with the problems of the West in general (the management of industrial civilization) and its relations both with the Soviet Union (capitalism vs. socialism) and with the third world (development vs. underdevelopment).

Taken as a whole, the West reveals in the realm of political philosophy the same trait characteristic of contemporary philosophy in general: a lack of agreement as to the methods and goal of philosophical reflection itself. Are the behavioral sciences replacing philosophy as the natural sciences have practically eliminated the philosophy of nature? Is the analysis of language, in politics as well, the essence of philosophy, so that preferences and choices may be a proper choice for analysis but not for rational determination? Is religion the only source of inspiration, the only way of transcending science or logical analysis? Or, on the contrary, is philosophy, with its own methods, still a valid form of investigating human nature and the meaning of history (or the nature of history and man's creation of his own humanity)?

When the subject of discussion is how to manage an already developed industrial society, men argue reasonably. When it becomes a question of comparing a pluralistic industrial society —a society with democratic institutions and guarantees of personal freedom—with a totalitarian industrial society, it is difficult not to prefer, at least in theory, the former (even admitting that a representative system is sometimes paralyzed and that, if economic growth and power is the goal, a totalitarian system is sometimes more efficient). Logical positivists and neo-Marxists or neo-Hegelians may mutually despise or at least misunderstand each other, but they generally agree that a government based on open discussion is preferable to one governed by the will of one man or a small group of men. And they also agree that this theoretical preference still does not make it possible to assert whether, in a given set of circumstances, what is preferable (open discussion) should be sacrificed to what is necessary (single-minded action).

Does the discussion of the meaning of philosophy relate to the discussion about the meaning of industrial society? I think it does. To stop wondering about the nature and purpose of man is an expression of blind faith in positivist science, or at least in science interpreted according to some kind of positivism. Yet at the same time, industrial society, the child of the scientific spirit, inevitably brings philosophy back into the picture, starting with the old Socratic questions: What good is the science of shipbuilding if you don't know how to navigate? What good is the science of navigation if you don't know where to go? What good are the sciences of geography or astronomy if you still won't know what to do at the other end of the world or in outer space? But which science will tell us what to do? None, answers the positivist. So be it; but if, beyond the pale of science, there is nothing but arbitrary decision, will the progress of science and scientific reason result in our handing over to the forces of irrationality our most basic concerns, that is, the definition and choice of what is essential, of what constitutes a good life and good society?

How could the West ever justify itself, either in its own eyes or the eyes of non-Westerners, if it were content with a science concerned only with the manipulation of natural forces and social beings and neglected the search for Reason which, beyond the realm of science or technique, is man's essential nature and his achievement throughout history?

BRIEF REMARKS ABOUT RAYMOND ARON'S TEXT

BY JEANNE HERSCH

It seems to me that this extremely interesting and provocative text has only one fault, which as a matter of fact is hard to define. It is a sort of working diagram which is so clear that anything connected with the confusion and welter of the social situation appears unintelligible and, as a result, unreal. Raymond Aron exposes a number of slogans and empties of their intellectual substance the pathetic objections used by many Westerners as the basis of both the best and the worst of their arguments pro and con. And yet these objections are facts, even if the reasons given for them are not. Often they imply, reflect, and mean something more real than the theories to which they refer.

For example, take the socialists and their slogan of "class struggle," which Raymond Aron refutes by citing the present situation in which both the equalitarian ideal and a planned economy are generally accepted. But he overlooks the fact that this situation was in large part created and imposed by the socialist-trade union struggle itself. It is not a matter of a pre-established harmony. And this past is not only a past: it helps to influence the present and the way men conceive of the future. It also no doubt indicates that today's unanimity may well be more verbal than real, that the terms "equality" or "planning" may embody radically different concepts—different enough at least so that when they are applied they give rise to very real conflicts.

I believe it is quite true that the traditional conflicts are today often sustained artificially. But, thank God, I do not believe in the unanimity of the West. The real problem is to discover the actual conflicts of our time and do something about them.

A few other remarks about specific points:

I do not believe we should compare people living under a communist government with the Western communists and ac-knowledge that the regime incarnates their ideology. I strongly doubt, for example, that it is correct to say about the Russians that communism was "the answer of a half-Western people . . ."

Nor do I think it is right to attribute the concern for freedom especially to the right.

I doubt that the communist regimes are really examples of rigid planning, and therefore efficient. I thought so for a long time—but this is not what I saw in Poland during the pre-Gomulka era.

Finally, the problems raised and the alternatives offered by the "third world" are, in my opinion, carried so far that a philo-sophical choice becomes impossible or scandalous—whereas here, as always (although on a scale unprecedented till now), philosophical choice must be sought in the often confused and uncertain arena where the demands of the present, plans for the future, and absolute values meet and struggle.

In short, while I accept without reservation many of the ques-tions raised by Raymond Aron, I would reproach him with having thrown such a clear light on the historical and social present that to a certain extent it distorts reality and modifies the practical possibilities. A question of method more than any-thing else.

The West in the Eyes of the Third World

(I am simply summing up a few ideas).

The third world is envious of the West. It wants to, and must, imitate it, follow in its footsteps, one day overtake it. *But it does not admire the West.*

This is not merely a question of the colonial past, but of the very character of our civilization. For the third world, Westerners are mere materialists whose mastery is due to the machines they were able to construct. It is imperative that the third world obtain these machines as soon as possible, and if possible learn how to copy them in order to build them itself. Therein lies the West's only claim to superiority. In the third world, certain peoples (the Hindus, for example) are convinced of their own spiritual superiority, and if it is necessary to imitate the West it is solely for reasons of basic necessities (food, etc.) which are of secondary importance. Others believe that the acquisition of technical mastery is the only real task and that anything which interferes (tradition, mores, beliefs) must be classed as dangerous and outmoded superstition. But everyone agrees in isolating the machines from the historical, philosophical, and religious context which allowed their invention. They even forget the nature of the work, the various efforts, the research implicit in technical progress, and, what is even more important, the nature of scientific research. Only "machines" interest them—complete, isolated, "in themselves."

This is one of the reasons why the third world often prefers the most recently developed machine rather than the one which would really contribute most to its social evolution.

If, in the eyes of the third world, the West appears stripped of its traditions, its efforts, and its age-old values, it is basically the West's own fault. We should not be surprised to find the third world ignorant of the spiritual roots and ramifications of the scientific and technical revolution if the West itself is unaware of or forgets them, or if it offers a mediocre picture of its adventure. Today in the West the sciences are still generally taught as a series of results, as a totality of objects of consumption, not as a creative process containing elements of risk, grief, detachment, and faith implicit in any creative act. Today, those in the West who worry about traditional values believe they have to look for a cure for "scientific and technical materialism" in the humanities, in teaching which diametrically opposes that of the sciences.

How can such a profound misunderstanding of the historical and philosophical bases of scientific and technical research by Westerners themselves not fail to give the third world a poor impression? If the West offers a cheap substitute rather than its true countenance, how can the third world be expected to discover it or be inspired by it?

The West misunderstands the origin, creative nature, and meaning of its own scientific and technical civilization. But for the moment, and in spite of so many violent upheavals, it is still living in the rich tradition of this origin, this creation, this meaning. That is why, for example, scholars who deny any free will for the individual still possess the fervent faith of earlier times in their search for truth. (No one knows how long such an involuntary transmission can last, and I do not believe that the impetus to science can be sustained for very long simply through the prestige of results obtained.) But in the third world the desire for the mere means of technical power does not engender the love of science and the values that feed it. Destroying native traditions, it runs the risk of putting nothing in their place, of creating a vacuum. And man abhors a vacuum.

It seems to me of the utmost importance, both for the West and for the third world, that a method of teaching the history of scientific ideas be developed, so that the spiritual sources of the research responsible for the amazing modern adventure would be made clear.

INDUSTRIAL SOCIETY IN SEARCH OF REASON

BY ERIC VOEGELIN

I. *The Pragmatic Pressure of Industrial Society*

1. The pressure toward pragmatic rationality of action derives basically from industrial technology. The pressure factors may be defined as follows:

a) Compared to earlier methods of production (in agriculture and manufacturing), the machine separates the worker from his tools. He can no longer produce by himself or in small groups.

b) The socialization of work, because production on a large scale is organized around a whole complex of machines and raw materials (this aspect of *de facto* socialization had already been noted by Marx).

c) The result is an increasing interdependence of the members of society.

d) The fact that everyone is dependent on the smooth functioning of the organization.

e) The assurance of an annual increase of productivity as soon as the organization has attained the sector of technical research.

Due to the pressure of the various factors, the following questions are, to an ever increasing degree, reduced to a simple pragmatic status:

(1) Ownership of the instruments of production.

(2) Planning—whether carried out by private companies or government agencies.

(3) Economic class status.

2. To these basic factors, which have a part in any national industrialized society, must be added those that apply specifically to Western Europe:

a) Industrial technology determines the optimum size of society as far as total exploitation is concerned.

b) The American and Russian societies fulfill the requirements as to size.

c) European national states are too small.

d) For technological reasons, the European common organization is a pragmatic necessity. It is also a condition for survival in a situation of power politics.

3. On the international scale, the most important pressure factor is "the bomb" as a means of mutual and radical destruction. It imposes the necessity of avoiding wars which would lead to the use of atomic bombs.

4. Pragmatic pressures and ideologies. The pragmatic pressure of the factors listed has not affected the structure of ideologies, but it has seriously diminished their credibility and their influence as a social factor. As a result, we can clearly see a growing area of basic agreement on questions of social organization. This consolidation has not always taken place because of a positive agreement on principles, but because of the pragmatic pressure which has removed many types of problems from the arena of political discussion by raising the specter of the terrible material consequences which threaten everyone alike.

II. *The Russian Problem*

1. Any discussion of Russian affairs requires that a distinction be made for the three following problems:

a) The creation of an industrial society competing with the West.

b) The institutional method of its creation, taking the time factor into consideration. Governmental despotism will probably produce the desired results faster than a free evolution would.

c) The rule of the Communist party with its immanentist eschatology.

2. Reality versus Ideology. The debate is vitiated by a lack of distinction between the ideological and scientific statements of the problem. According to the ideological declaration, as it appears in the Soviet constitution, the Russian problem must be thought of in the following terms:

a) The Soviet Union is a socialist society.

b) Its political regime is a temporary dictatorship of the proletariat.

c) Its goal is the establishment of a communist society, of the kingdom of freedom in the Marxian sense.

Reversing the order would give the following scientific counterdeclarations:

a) It is impossible to establish a communist society in the Marxian sense, because this symbol is the immanentist hypostasis of a transcendent eschaton.

b) There is no dictatorship of the proletariat in the Soviet Union. A sectarian community imposes its despotic rule on a people who, by the contingencies of its history, has shown itself incapable of establishing a representative form of government in the Western sense of the term.

c) An industrial society, characterized by co-operative and state ownership of the instruments of production, is in the process of being developed.

3. Viewpoints to be taken into consideration:

a) "The pragmatic pressure of industrial society will to a large extent reduce the sector of problems in which the ideological nonmeaning can possibly influence or affect the rational functioning of the organization." This is certainly a tenable opinion, but it does not follow that pressure will affect either the institutional methods (despotic) or social ascendancy of the communist eschatology.

b) "Communist eschatology will die of an atrophy of faith unless the communist realm is not established after a certain length of time." In the long run, this opinion will also doubtless be valid, but the period of time may well be very long. The following arguments can be advanced in favor of this reservation:

(1) Lenin anticipated criticism concerning the nonrealization of communist society by suggesting that it might take a century or two.

(2) The argument of a hostile imperialist world.

(3) The limited success in building the industrial society. The West had been living the myth of "Progress" for two hundred years before realizing that it was really material progress and stopping to ask itself: "Is that all there is to it?"

c) The imponderable factor: the spiritual and intellectual life of the Russian people:

(1) How much longer can a young generation which has grown up under the system bear the weary annihilation of spiritual life?

(2) How long can the irrationality of communist ideology resist the growing pressures of rationality in the industrial sector of the society?

III. *Reason and Society*

1. The postulates of classical politics:

a) Man participates in the Logos or transcendent Nous.

b) The life of reason consists of actualizing this participation and making it sufficiently important so that it becomes an influence on the development of character.

c) In regard to the life of reason, men are potentially equal, but empirically (for whatever reason) they are unequal in the application of their potentiality.

d) Men capable of an optimum application are a minority in every society.

e) A society has a *de facto* hierarchical structure in terms of actualizing the life of reason.

f) The "quality" of society depends on the degree to which the life of reason, actively carried out by a minority of its members, becomes a creative force in that society.

2. Additional postulates: A number of other assumptions must be added to the classic postulates. These were of course

implicit in the politics of Plato and Aristotle, but only became explicit at a later date.

a) The psychic tension of the life of reason is difficult for the majority of the members of a society to bear.

b) As a result, any society in which the life of reason has reached a high degree of differentiation has a tendency to develop, along with the life of reason, a "mass belief." By sheer social expansion, mass belief may reduce the life of reason to socially meaningless enclaves or even forcefully suppress it.

c) In the case of early Jewish society, Jeremiah diagnosed this tendency as the "fall" of the people away from the "true God" to "false gods." At the height of the spiritual flowering of the Middle Ages in the West, Joachim de Flore conceived of a "Third Realm" in the framework of history, and this has, with a certain number of variations, become an element of mass beliefs in the West today.

Plato was aware of the problem when, for reasons of political expediency, he made concessions to the "popular myth" and accepted it as a parallel to existence in philosophical form. Examples prove that mass beliefs can assume many different forms. When the situation is favorable, as in the cases of the Hebrews and Greeks, the people can retain, or revert to, a living polytheistic myth; when, as at the height of the Middle Ages in the West, no living myth exists, the search for a mass belief is directed toward immanentist symbols of the apocalyptic or secularist-ideological type.

d) The co-existence of mass beliefs and the life of reason in a society has, since the Stoics, been classified under the headings of *theologia civilis* and *theologia naturalis*.

e) The rise of ideologies to social and political power in modern society must be considered in the context of attempts to establish a civil theology.

IV. *Western Civil Theology*

Western society emerged from the Middle Ages without a civil theology for the masses of the growing national states; even less likely is there to be discovered in the heritage of the

past a civil theology for the industrial society which has tran-
scended the limits of the national state. The efforts to cope
with this problem have brought to light certain systems:

1. The Gelasian System. Included among the varieties of
the Gelasian system should be included all the attempts to adapt
the division of temporal and spiritual powers to the changing
demands of philosophy, the national states, and ideologies. The
succession of representative examples is the following:

a) Gelasius: Emperor-Pope

b) Dante: Emperor-Philosopher (Averroist)

c) Bodin: National Sovereign-Philosopher (Mystic)

d) Comte: Industrial Manager-Positivist Intellectual (Ideology)

2. The Minimum Dogma. In order to satisfy the masses
and at the same time protect the life of reason, philosophers have
tried to distill from the life of reason a series of dogmas which
everyone is supposed to believe, leaving the masses free to adopt
any other beliefs, so long as they do not conflict with the minimum dogma. Spinoza wanted to have the minimum dogma instituted as a state cult, with the proviso that those people whose
emotional life was not satisfied by the bare minimum be au-
thorized to establish more elaborate private dogmas and cults.
The precedent for Spinoza's construction is found in the Platonic attempt to outline an obligatory minimum dogma in the
Laws.

3. The attempts of sectarian communities to impose by force
their immanentist beliefs on a society as a state cult. The principal examples are:

a) the Puritan Revolution

b) the French Revolution

c) the National-Socialist Revolution

d) the Communist Revolution

4. The Civil Government in the Lockean sense. A "natural"
political sphere should be separated from the life of reason and
spirit. This "natural" sphere has the monopoly of being public.
Hence there will be no state cult; churches and sects are reduced

to the status of private associations. In order to make this construction valid, Locke had to establish a careful equilibrium between tolerance and intolerance. On the one hand, the civil government allows complete freedom to the life of reason and spirit, together with its social manifestations; on the other hand, sects and ideologies which insist on making a political issue of their faith cannot be tolerated (Catholics, Mohammedans, Antinomians, and Levellers were denied civil status). The civil government operates on the premise that the way of life of a liberal-protestant community must and will become the way of life of the nation.

5. Constitutional Democracy. Based to a large extent on the Lockean concept of civil government (but less rigidly constructed, so that it could absorb the problems of industrial society), this system has been practiced in Western governments, and especially in the Anglo-Saxon countries. In order to operate, it presupposes that the constitution itself is in a way an article of faith, that "constitutional democracy" is the predominant mass creed, the civil theology of the society. If this condition is fulfilled, the society can be "pluralistic" to the extent that free rein is given the residues of intellectual and spiritual movements (churches, sects, ideologies, and, last but not least, philosophy), assuming that they will live side by side without subverting the constitutional structure. The strength of constitutional democracy, especially in the Anglo-Saxon countries, is the eschatological tension left over from the Puritan Revolution which endows the constitutional form with a character of "finality" as the successful experiment in organizing a society with a classical and Christian tradition.

V. *The Good Society*

The "good society" is a concept of classical politics which requires considerable refurbishing if we are to use it to analyze contemporary politics. According to the classical concept, the "good society" is one which:

(1) is large enough and wealthy enough to make the life of

reason possible, at least for the minority capable of putting this human potentiality to work;

(2) is organized in such a way that the life of reason becomes a social force in a society's culture, including its political affairs.

The concept also bears the burden of two assumptions which have become debatable in our time:

a) that a society, in order to be good, should not be any larger than a polis;

b) the fact that a sizable percentage of men in every society are slaves by nature justifies the institution of slavery and, in general, the maltreatment of those who are scarcely capable of facing up to the responsibilities of citizenship.

The second assumption can be dismissed out of hand, since it has been replaced by the Jewish-Christian concept of man as the image of God, of man's dignity and inviolability regardless of how society may judge his conduct or value. But the first assumption requires closer consideration.

1. First, we must clear up a point which in our ideological environment is too easily obscured. A good, or even an excellent society in the classic sense by no means means an ideal society. The Platonic-Aristotelian paradigms take into consideration the fact that men are unequal in actualizing their equal natures; the structure of society is in fact, for unknown reasons, hierarchical and not equalitarian, and we know of no way of changing this situation.

The classical political thinkers were realists. Most of their modern colleagues are not.

Two corollaries must be added:

a) The model of the good society is not an a priori datum. Its construction is extremely elastic and must vary with our empirical knowledge of human nature and society. One sure thing is that the social effectiveness of the life of reason, which is constantly developing, must be included. For the rest, the field of construction is wide open—as is proved by Plato's readiness to consider second, third, and fourth best paradigms, to none of which he would deny the title of "good society." The problem of the "good society" evolves into that of setting up a scale of societies with varying degrees of goodness.

b) The title "good society" does not contain any eschatological overtones; its establishment is not a final achievement which brings imperfect history to an end. Even the best of the good societies follows, according to the classical concept, the cyclical law of decline and fall and its corruption begins from the moment of its inception. Or, in noncyclical modern terms: the idea of a good society is incompatible with the ideological dreams of a terrestrial paradise that will last forever.

2. The question of size poses a delicate problem. According to the classical concept, modern societies are not good because they are too large and do not allow the citizens to participate fully in public affairs. This notion cannot be dismissed out of hand as preposterous; some excellent authorities today, Leo Strauss for one, think it is valid. At the other extreme from this radical view may be listed the factors which were nonexistent in antiquity and which today make possible the building of a good society on the vast scale required by industrial society. Among them are: better organization of transportation and communications, the development of representative government and federalism and, last but not least, Christianity, thanks to which the meaning of human existence is no longer circumscribed by its expression in political life. Nevertheless, anyone who has had the opportunity of observing life in the provinces of a large country—with its accumulation of resentment and frustrations, the sense of being left out, neglected, of having failed, the attendant warping of the mind and the development of a ghetto atmosphere—will have to admit that the very size of society creates problems which require a great deal of attention and adequate treatment.

The problems of size, which prejudice the "goodness" of any modern industrial society, have become of prime importance on the international level because the material standard of living of Western societies is universally accepted as the condition of a "good society." With the acceptance of these standards the underdeveloped countries have, from the psychological point of view, been transformed into provinces of a world society whose center is in the West and especially in the United States. The problems of communism, for example, have in political practice assumed a very peculiar form, not at all inherent in the dogma, because the Soviets have concentrated all their efforts on building an industrial society whose efficiency and productivity will be comparable to those of the United States.

3. The problem of viability is closely connected with that of size. To be good, a society must first of all exist, and "goodness" is itself no guarantee. With the arrival of the era of empires the city-state was doomed. If we were to accept without qualification the classical concepts it would follow not only that industrial societies are worthless but that, in the age of industrial societies, "good societies" can survive only if they are tolerated by the major powers which are not terribly "good." Therefore the question of "goodness" cannot be treated without reference to the historical conditions of social existence, and we must once again study the "pragmatic pressure" of industrial society from the viewpoint of its influence on the life of reason.

The development of modern science, technology, and industry is a historical process, and as such not at everyone's disposal. The romantic revolt and the dream of returning to the simple life make no sense at all; no one would think of advising the underdeveloped countries to remain in their happy state and be glad they had escaped the fate of industrialization. The general agreement on this point is more than a consensus on the level of materialism; it can be justified rationally by the results of industrialization in Western society as we have been able to observe them. It is evident that in its initial stage industrialization caused social evils which in turn engendered ideological revolts, so that Western progress seemed to be self-defeating. Moreover, the social nightmare of that period still weighs menacingly over the West, for it materialized in a monstrous way through communism and its political consolidation in Russia. And yet in the internal development of Western society the later stages of industrialization have strengthened rather than weakened the Western experiment in constitutional democracy. Since Western society is in fact "good" to the extent that it has absorbed and preserved the classical and Christian traditions, it was exposed to the serious danger of destruction from within by the immanentist ideologies. The expansion of industrial society during the present century has, because of the pragmatic pressure previously mentioned, eliminated a large number of—if not all—irritations from the area of serious discussion on an emotional level. Therefore the chances of preserving a "good society" have substantially improved. We have been granted a sort of reprieve, and are obligated to use it to the utmost to repair the damage which the age of ideologies has inflicted on Western substance.

4. In the West, constitutional democracy as a constitutional form is so closely allied with the notion of the good society that we must note a strong tendency to forget, both in theory and practice, that "goodness" is the quality of a society and not of a governmental form. When society is good it can function under the form of a constitutional democracy; when it is not good, it cannot. Thus a society which is not qualified for this governmental form can easily start down the road to disaster if it adopts a Western-type constitution. Unconscionable damage to millions of people throughout the world has resulted from ill-considered constitutional experiments modeled after the West. It's imperative that we face the facts. Not all societies are good, and the attempt to imitate the Western type entails revolutionary changes which can perhaps only be brought about by dubious means. The problem, although it has become in our time particularly acute, is not a new one. The classics were well aware that "goodness" cannot be exported. In the nineteenth century, John Stuart Mill in his *Essay on Liberty* limited representative institutions to those societies in which the life of reason and rational debate were sufficiently developed, while for "barbarian" societies he recommended "despotism" as the form of government best suited to improving them. It is only in the twentieth century that we

have developed that fateful blindness to the fact that a good society is something that must grow historically and that this growth is painful. If we take into account historical dynamics (a problem that was *not* taken into account by the classics), and especially contemporary dynamics, the question of "goodness" will require a certain amount of revision and refinement. We must admit that constitutional democracy may be a terrible form of government for an Asian or African country, whereas some form of enlightened despotism, autocracy, or military dictatorship can be the best if we believe that the rulers are using this means to try to create a good society. It will not be an easy matter to judge or give concrete advice. At one extreme, the sanguinary dictatorship of a Stalin is no longer deemed good even by the Russians. But if the mild rule of a Nehru results in the fantastic and irremediable disaster which, if we are to believe the Ford Foundation report, will overtake India in a few years, that will scarcely be considered "good" either.

These thoughts give rise to some unpleasant questions. Will the impact of the West on an Asiatic civilization such as India result in disaster and terrible suffering over a long period of time before the situation can be brought under control? Is rapid industrialization, copied from the West, always the best means of achieving a good society? Is it ever the best means? For, historically, industrial society has evolved in the West within the framework of rationalism. Can the historical order of cause and effect be reversed—as a certain Marxist precept holds—and the good society be expected to rise as the superstructure above industrialization? Shouldn't the process of industrialization in societies where it is not indigenous be accompanied by profound changes if certain unexpected and perhaps undesirable results are to be avoided? For the moment we shall have to leave these questions unanswered.

5. The essential nucleus of a good society—without which it is worthless no matter what its accomplishments may be in other areas—is the life of reason. In order to make this notion useful for political analysis, we must make a distinction between ra-

tional action in areas peripheral to the human psyche and action which affects the central order of the psyche itself. I shall therefore distinguish between pragmatic and noetic reason, pragmatic reason being understood as all rational action in the sciences of the external world, the development of technology, and the co-ordination of means and ends as they apply to the external world, whereas noetic reason includes all rational action in the sciences of man, society, and history, both in the formation of the order of the psyche and of society. These two areas of rational action are relatively independent of each other. Any society, even the most primitive, includes an area of pragmatic rationality, since without the rational action which provides the means of existence there would be no society. The development of pragmatic rationality is, in any event, quite compatible with a high degree of irrationality in the sphere of noetic reason—*homo faber* corresponds perfectly well with Levy-Bruhl's "prelogical" mentality of the primitive—and ideological governments can build industrial societies. Conversely, a highly developed life of reason in the noetic sense—in the Athens of Aeschylus or Plato—does not necessarily lead to the expansion of the sciences of the external world.

6. Before the notion of the life of reason in the noetic sense can be applied a further distinction must be made. The difficulties of rational debate on an international scale arise from two different types of irrationality which are supposed to become our partners in a debate of this kind:

a) In some civilizations, such as India and China, the life of reason has never extricated itself completely from the cosmological myth. Even if there is a small group of leaders capable of carrying on a rational discussion in the Western sense of the term, the masses are still living at a less differentiated cultural level.

b) In the West a very different type of irrationality—that of ideologies—has developed. They all have in common the denial of the *participation,* the *methexis,* in transcendent reason as the source of the life of reason; all of them have these derivative characteristics to the extent that they are immanentist perversions of a life of reason which is already historically differentiated.

7. The application of the concept to our problem of rational debate would require a complicated and careful casuistry. A few typical examples are:

a) In Western society, our first difficulty concerns the intellectuals and the ideologies they represent. Debate in the true sense of the term is impossible, because they refuse to discuss the basic problems of the life of reason; the immanentist position must be accepted without question. The only result of any attempt to draw the ideological intellectual into a debate will be the use of techniques which consist of skirting the issue or reiterating the premises as if they had never been questioned, and apologetic rhetoric (although the long-term results of such attempts are of course incalculable). The difficulties of debate are still widely prevalent in Western society, although there has been some change in the course of the last generation; the hard core of resistance can be found today on the level of the mass media of communications, especially in the United States, while the academic sphere shows a notable improvement. It seems that the age of ideologies is drawing to a close—for reasons inherent in the structure of these ideologies which cannot be discussed here in detail. This process of exhaustion is accelerated by the "pragmatic pressure" already mentioned.

b) In the debate with Russia there do not seem to be any obstacles on the level of pragmatic reason, that is, in the mathematical sciences and in power politics—the argument of the "bomb" is fully understood. Difficulties arise in sciences where Marxist ideology has been able to make itself felt—the Lysenko affair is sufficient proof. In philosophical matters there seems no possibility of discussion. In its interpretation of man, society, and history, communist ideology remains an untouchable, inaccessible block which is not open to question.

c) As for those civilizations which have not completely emerged from the culture of the myth, serious difficulties arise on the pragmatic level. It would appear that the techniques have not yet been found which will convince the Indian masses in a short period of time that cattle should be eaten rather than allowed to run rampant through the fields, that the caste system should be eliminated and that habits of diet should be modified— not to mention the difficulties encountered in trying to inculcate rational habits of organization and administration.

d) A special problem has grown up during the height of the age of ideology through the education in Western universities of the elite of the underdeveloped countries. Besides out-and-out communism, we should also mention that strange cocktail of Rousseau-Marx-John Dewey, with a dash of neo-positivism and British analysis, which was given to non-European students as the very essence of Western culture. Just as our corruption of the nineteenth century now comes home to us with a vengeance in the form of Russian communism, so in the course of the past two generations we have studiously built up centers of intellectual resistance to the life of reason in China and India, in the Arab countries, and in Africa. The effects of this unfortunate period of Western "education" will plague us for a long time to come.

e) These last remarks lead us back of the position of the West in the present conflict. What do we have to offer by way of guidance or leadership in this world-wide transformation of society? The answer is: everything and nothing. We know what the life of reason and the good society are; we can cultivate the former and try, by our actions, to bring about the latter. We can restate the problem: the formation of the psyche by encouraging participation in transcendent reason—which is what I have done, in however brief and imperfect way, in this paper. And that is all one can do; whether or not this offer is accepted depends on the Spirit that blows where It pleases. Collectively, as a society, there is at the moment little, if anything, we can do. For the dissemination of knowledge on a massive scale is the province of institutions, and what we disseminate by institutional means, be they the media of mass communication or academic organizations, may perhaps do more harm than good.

To be sure, the ideologies have not been able to destroy the life of reason in the West, but the damage is serious—even though we hide it under the euphemism of "pluralistic society." If everything goes well, it will take at least a generation before the Western stables are clean enough to make the power of the West, which rests on its life of reason, institutionally visible and persuasive once again.

THE RELATIONSHIP BETWEEN THOUGHT AND ACTION IN THE THREE WORLDS

BY CHARLES MORAZÉ

However sweeping the powers of a chief of state, he does not have real freedom of action. His actions are controlled by a number of powerful factors, some of which are inherent in the society, others in his own personality, all of which reflect the exigencies both of the general conditions and the prevailing circumstances of the action.

Any man in a position of high authority will already have held subordinate positions in government or in a political party and undergone certain trials which will have trained his sensibility and reason. He then becomes more interested in some problems than others and solves them according to the education or training he has received. It is true that the exercise of authority in itself provides the statesman with opportunities for liberating himself to some extent from the consequences of this restraint, but never enough to modify his personality.

Moreover, the fact that this personality was selected for the exercise of power is an indication that it could be relied upon to single out the most pressing problems and find appropriate solutions for them, that is, the solutions easiest to understand and put into effect by the most important people concerned. Between the person in power and the people who put him there and now support and help him there arises a long series of actions and reactions which condition—in the strict sense that social psychologists give this term—the statesman's activities.

It seems to me that one of the chief lessons we can learn from the new humanistic sciences is this strong limitation imposed on the concept of freedom and of conscience. We are not free to think or act in accordance with the truth, but only in accordance with what we have been taught and what we have been allowed. And this limitation is all the more serious in that we increasingly believe we are acting freely, whereas we are blindly obeying the dictates of our own personality, dictates it transmits after having assimilated them from the education or training to which it has unconsciously been subjected.

Thus it is impossible for the adviser of a statesman to induce him to carry out any measures which are too far from the area and lines of action established during this conditioning process. And it is useless for a thinker to hope to establish real contact with authority unless he himself is prepared a priori to indulge in this game of reciprocal influences.

Therefore, instead of trying to influence action directly, thought should act rather on education, through information: that is its proper role. Thought is better suited to create authority than to advise it.

Just how well it fulfills this function will of course depend on how quickly and accurately it discovers what problems and solutions the men it steers toward power will be called upon to cope with. This effort to look ahead becomes all the more imperative as the changes of the human condition and social structures take place more and more rapidly. Forecasting is becoming one of the essential methods of the new humanistic studies.

Forecasting was neither necessary nor even useful in the days when the conditions of action were subject to only slight change and often remained identical for several generations. There was no problem for education to prepare future action in the light of present conditions. It would seem that by the nineteenth century the relationship between education and action had already changed considerably and it was becoming necessary to establish closer contacts between discovery and education. Meanwhile, information had to rid itself of the shackles of tradition in order to be able to prepare for action in keeping with fairly rapid changes of circumstance. It was at this time that freedom of information became an integral part of the modern state, as it was conceived in what we call the Western democracies.

The advantage of this freedom of information is that it allows a good deal of latitude in choosing the various concepts of man's destiny for the purposes of education. We can accept Mannheim's estimate that certain of these concepts will always remain utopian, while others are destined to become ideologies. The former are those which will never be put into effect and therefore not be utilized by authority, while the latter will provide useful guidance for the same authority. The wide variety of ideologies makes it possible to formulate a number of different programs, parties, or teams with sufficient latitude so that, depending upon the exigencies, now one will prevail, now another. This procedure is flexible enough to fit in perfectly with the necessities of action.

This same freedom of information does have one drawback, however: it assumes an educational effort on a wide enough scale so that several teams will be formed simultaneously in a single country. It also assumes that the mechanisms for transferring the power from one team to another are sufficiently flexible to avoid any violent shocks. This comparative abundance of resources and this flexibility in the transference of power can only be found in relatively privileged countries. It requires in particular that the loss of power does not entail so great a reduction of personal status that those in power refuse to relinquish it. It also requires that the economic sectors, as distinguished from the civil service, provide possibilities for satisfactory careers. The statutory separation of the economic and political systems is a wise one and provides encouragement for liberalism of thought and action. But it is a costly division.

One wonders whether nations which, having been poor so long, must grow rich quickly, may not be compelled to economize their resources to such an extent that there is no room for a multiplicity of ideologies and parties. This is especially so because the control of power tends to imply the control of wealth as well, so that the opposition is naturally tempted to assume a revolutionary attitude. The greater the appetite for progress, the greater the need of forecasting, so that all efforts are concentrated and oriented toward a single "scientifically" calculated goal. This method of rational forecasting first developed most easily within the framework of Marxism.

This rational forecasting caused the cadres of primitive Marxism to burst, while it developed extensively and with increasing subtlety in the liberal nations. But the institutions set up in the Soviet Union for the diffusion of information are still dominated by the concern to economize the available resources. Instead of commercial advertising, which is deemed wasteful both because of its cost and the competition it causes among a variety of products, the Russians substitute the state store and the single product for every need. The overriding concern to provide tools of the highest quality in the shortest possible time tempts them to ignore details. Construction will proceed at a more rapid pace if targets are fixed in advance so that the simple tasks can be distributed without any possibility of choice. There is, of course, the risk of erroneous planning, and there thus must be established an uninterrupted flow of information between the leaders and those who carry out their orders. During the violent era of economic planning, the Soviet press had two main objectives: the publication on page one of letters to Stalin pointing out to the authorities any concrete difficulties encountered; the replies to these letters in the form of directives, sometimes accompanied by the inevitable autocriticism.

From below, only criticism bearing on practical points is tolerated, for the single ideology is defined from above. The sole purpose of this ideology is to encourage the worship of "the practical" in the lower echelons by confining its praise to Marxist materialism.

Faced with these two widely varying systems of the West and the East—the former maintaining the necessary multiplicity of ideologies and the latter championing the system of a single ideology—which one will the "third world" choose? Because it has to build a powerful industrial society as fast as possible, it is tempted by material efficiency, but an ideological variety is more in keeping with the deep-rooted aspirations of peoples whose worship has been directed toward a multiple reflection of the Divine. This makes the spiritual position of the West a difficult one. By singing the praise of the secular and of technical progress, it is paving the road for a form of Marxism.

The alternative is to discover some new proposition which, by reinterpreting the ancient myths, can find something better than technical progress to offer an avid world.

Discussions

INTRODUCTION: THE CONCEPT OF
INDUSTRIAL SOCIETY

ARON: As you know, the Congress for the Freedom of Culture has organized a whole series of meetings and conducted
research under the general heading of "Tradition and Change."
What linked together and inspired this research was the idea
that all societies, both those we call developed and those we call
underdeveloped, are experiencing at the present time a conflict
between their traditions and the rapid changes that growth entails. We had thought, when we began, that if the clash was more
violent between tradition and modernism in the underdeveloped
countries, it also existed in the so-called developed societies of
the West. The theme "Tradition and Change" became as it were
the over-all title for a whole series of investigations, which resulted in three seminars: the Tokyo seminar, which dealt with
the problems of economic development in the underdeveloped
countries; the second, which was devoted to the present and
future changes in Soviet society; and the third, which dealt with
the representative institutions in new nations. I had been struck
by the fact that these three seminars paid practically no attention to the West and concerned itself basically with the possible
or actual westernization of non-Western societies. The seminar
on economic development attempted to determine under what
conditions so-called underdeveloped countries could attain a
social and economic structure comparable to that of Western
societies; the seminar on the Soviet society often gave me the

impression that the question raised was: When will Soviet society finally resemble Western society, that is, will it persist in refusing to recognize its affinity with the West or will it discover it as times goes by? Will the Soviet world grow increasingly "liberal" in accordance with our hopes and ideals? Finally, the third seminar was directly concerned with the possibility of transferring Western political institutions. At Rhodes we questioned to what extent non-Western societies are able and desirous of introducing—at the same time as they assimilate modern technology and economics—the liberal democratic institutions which we consider characteristic of Western politics. The fact that these three seminars were devoted to the problems of relations between the West and the non-West or the problems of transferring Western institutions to the non-Western world made me ask myself the following question: Shouldn't the West take a long hard look at itself? For these three seminars assumed, with a certain, perhaps justified, naïveté, that the West was sufficiently sure of itself so that it could examine its possible universalization without at the same time examining itself, asking just what it was. I tried to come up with some answers to the question of why there had not been a seminar on the West itself, and found three. Two have already been mentioned in my report. There is also a third, which can serve as my point of departure.

If the West often seems to assume that it has no reason to examine or question itself, it is because, in spite of appearances, the West is taken as a criterion or model by a large part of humanity. I might even say by that same humanity which curses it. After all, the society most openly hostile to the West, the Soviet Union, has as its slogan: "Overtake the United States." And for me nothing is more striking than the fact that the "Marxists" of the Soviet Union have no trouble reconciling their theories about the historical advance of the Soviet regime over the West and their own economic lag. For, by strict Marxist dogma, the combination of a regime's advance and its lag in the development of its forces of production is quite inconceivable. In Marx's Marxism, it is impossible for a regime which is socially, politically, and intellectually ahead to be economically behind. We non-Marxists have no trouble at all accepting this contradiction. But Marxists should have a great deal of trouble accepting it, for this implies a rupture in the parallelism between the technical-economic evolution on the one hand and the social and political, or intellectual, evolution on the other. Not only is the American economy used as a model in a certain sense by the Soviet economy, but I believe that a great number of countries which are manifestly anti-Western accept implicitly the exemplary value of Western scientific, technical, and economic institutions. If we have not delved deeply enough into what is problematical in our own societies, we have perhaps been influenced by the way in which such a large part of the world, even though it berates or upbraids us, implicitly recognizes that it wants to move down the same road we have taken. It is quite obvious that even though American technology and economy are cited as models, it does not follow automatically that the political institutions of the United States are similarly accepted. But even on this point I tend to believe that the West is given greater recognition, more acceptance, than the propaganda speeches might lead us to believe. For in the final analysis such words as "democracy" and "liberty" belong to the universalized vocabulary of our time. All propaganda and ideology aside, it is nevertheless difficult to admit logically that a regime with a single, monolithic state party is more liberal than one with several parties and open ideological discussion. I am well aware that, from an ideological point of view, one can say anything and justify anything. But to my mind the majority of those who say it are not all that convinced.

Besides this reason—the fact that the West is taken as a model by a large part of humanity—there are, I believe, two other reasons why the West has not investigated itself. One of these reasons was mentioned in the beginning of my report when I spoke of the "pacified or established democracies" and the weakening or lessening of ideological quarrels, and the second near the end when I noted that, to a large extent, the West does

not really know what its own political philosophy is, and perhaps even what its authentic human and moral goal may be,
beyond mere economic growth, which is accepted as an obvious
necessity.

Since my whole paper is based on a certain notion of industrial
society, which I have more or less taken for granted, it seems
to me worth while at the start of these discussions to dwell on
this notion, which is fast becoming a classic one in Western
thought. I might add that Professor Rostow's famous articles,
to which *The Economist* devoted fourteen pages—and that is
practically unique in the annals of the last hundred years—presuppose the idea of the industrial society which I am presenting
here. For these articles suggest that all modern societies—at least
from the economic, social, and even political point of view—
belong to a same type, are moving along the same path, and
are strung out along that common path in varying positions of
progress. This method of viewing modern societies implies that
all existing societies belong to the same social type—the type
I call industrial society—which I think we should discuss at least
briefly.

I should first like to say that, historically speaking, this concept comes, I believe, from Auguste Comte. But I should like
to add that I did not borrow it from Comte, but from him through
another source. I believe that the point of view expressed in
Professor Rostow's articles is a direct, logical, and inevitable
consequence of the thought of Colin Clark. I think that the entire
postwar movement—the economy of development, the economy
of growth, phase of growth, stages reached by expanding economies—this whole economic viewpoint comes straight out of
Colin Clark and his fundamental work, *Conditions of Economic
Progress.* In this book, Colin Clark did not expound the concept
of the industrial society. But his method of classifying economies
—whether socialist or capitalist, Soviet or Western—along a
single path, the stages of which were marked by total production
or per capita production or production per worker or by productivity, this method of situating all economies on a single path

obviously presupposed that there was a new type of modern economy to which all contemporary societies belonged or wished to belong. Wished to or ought to, I leave the question open, for it is conceivable that in some cases it was a matter of free choice, in others of constraint. There are two ways in which Colin Clark implied this philosophy which Professor Rostow expounded: first, by introducing the five stages of development—which may be open to debate—and second by trying to establish a relationship, using a very Marxist method, between a large number of social and even political phenomena and the stages of development.

As for the concept of industrial society, I found in the work of Auguste Comte—to which I had been led by Colin Clark—a definition which seemed to me, at bottom, unusually adapted to our current way of thinking. For Comte, you will recall, does not define industrial society by the industry; for him, it is not the creation of large factories or industrial concentrations which characterizes this society, but rather the following essential features: first, the freedom of work for the individual. Workers are free, not trapped in a hereditary condition or condemned to remain where they happened to be born. Second, everyone's place in society is determined basically by the function he fulfills in the total or collective work picture. Hierarchy and values are established by this functional organization of work and society. Finally, work is transformed by the systematic application of science to the organization of production. Now, it appears to me that in the final analysis these three characteristics of industrial society—individual freedom, functionalization of the social organization, and the scientific rationalization of work —remain valid today and enable us to understand that the introduction of the industrial society is not a quantitative, formal phenomenon, but the transformation of human attitudes and social organization; the increase in production, measured quantitatively, is the expression and symbol of this transformation, not the basic reality. At the present time, industrial society is defined by a number of perfectly acceptable criteria: urbanization, industrialization, life expectancy, a decrease in the percentage of the total labor force employed in agriculture. All these immediately visible characteristics are acceptable, but I believe that Comte's definition explains phenomena which naive sociological observation merely notes or records.

This said, I hasten to add that, in my opinion, the concept of "Industrial Society" must be utilized in keeping with a method I would call interrogative and not dogmatic. By that I mean that I do not know—and probably none of us knows—just how extensive are the inevitable political, social, and intellectual implications of this new social structure. It would be Marxist in the worse sense of the term to assume that the entire political and social organization will be transformed by the industrial society, or, worse yet, that it would be the same in all industrial societies. What does seem to me worth while and necessary is to ascertain the inherent characteristics of this type of society in order to try to find what new problems it raises, in what way it may affect the old, established political problems. And it would obviously be wrong to overlook the differences which must continue to exist no matter what the origin of the industrial society might be. I shall list only the most obvious differences: this industrial society will appear concretely different depending on the geographic conditions of the specific group under review. There is no reason why customs or social and religious beliefs should be identical in all industrial societies. The diversity of social organization is in no way eliminated by the common structural characteristics of various industrial societies. Finally, the industrial society which is now being transferred was not the same in the first half of the nineteenth century as in the second half, and it is different still in the present century. Consequently, the phenomena of transferring economic and technical organization are not the same, depending on the degree of scientific or technical development attained by the country in question.

I am also convinced—and this was implicit in my report— that industrial society represents in the history of humanity an original social type, with implications of considerable importance. I shall offer only two "proofs," neither of which is convincing, but certainly intriguing. It seems obvious to me that the nature of industrial society profoundly modifies the traditional style of two of man's most basic activities: work and war. If it is true, as I believe, that neither work (or production) nor war can, in a fully developed industrial society, be what they were during the several thousand years of the historical phase, it seems almost inevitable to me that we are heading toward, or are already in, a new type of society. This does not mean that many of the philosophical problems are not exactly the same as in the past. But to take only the case of war from the moment man first acquired the capacity of massive destruction —and probably destruction of the whole human race—I submit that something genuinely new has resulted from this fact, and that is the impossibility, or the absurdity, of a war to the finish, a total war. I might even say that there is no longer any rational total war; and that is new. For throughout history total victories were rational, under certain circumstances. The moderation of war was reasonable; it was not necessarily rational. And now we are entering a world in which the only war which might still be rational would be a limited war, one that would not involve the major powers. Starting with this concept of industrial society, I thought we might try to grasp the total or over-all complex of problems of our time.

I must admit that the purpose of my report, and of this entire week of discussions, is to try to do what we increasingly hesitate to undertake, that is, ponder the whole philosophical-historical complex of problems in which we live.

Why, in my opinion, does this concept give us a chance to think on a world-wide scale? Because I believe this concept enables us to understand the unity-plurality of contemporary man and the unity-plurality of the philosophical-political problems we face. Unity-plurality of man—you can see right away what I am thinking: on the one hand, relations among different societies have never been so close or intense as they are today.

There is a greater flow of communication between China, Japan, India, the United States, and Europe than ever before in the history of the world. The Indian peasant knows more about the English laborer, and vice versa, than at any other period. In this sense there is a greater human unity than ever before. But at the same time living conditions are different than they have ever been. A few centuries ago, the living conditions of an Indian peasant and an English peasant were not so very different. Today those differences are enormous. And third, there is a strange multiplicity of ideologies. For in certain respects this type of society which is spreading is the same, but neither side accepts the basic affinity. The Soviets would be somewhat put out at the way I pose the problem, and many of my colleagues and young Marxists in Paris dislike the way I state problems, because it deprives the Society of their choice of this seal of absolute originality and total value. Thus, in one way, mankind is both more united and more divided than ever before. More united by communication and more divided because the inequalities of living conditions increase with the stages of development of industrial society and also because beliefs and creeds today are primarily oriented toward the very organization of society. If we want to discuss Marxist ideology from a relative point of view, we are in a sense destroying the state orthodoxy of the Soviet Union. Thus it suffices to be scientific—as I believe I am and you doubtless believe you are—in studying the reality of Soviet society, to be aggressive. This combination of man's unity-plurality is reflected, I believe, in the unity-plurality of world problems, and explains the wide range of subjects covered in my report.

I did not raise so many problems for fear that we might lack for subject matter, but rather because I believe they derive from a common source. When we discuss Western society and Soviet society, we are discussing the margin of economic and political variation possible within the same type of industrial society. When we discuss the West and the underdeveloped countries, we are discussing the possibility of transferring Western technical, economic, and eventually political institutions to countries of another civilization. When we have finished debating these so-called sociological or positive problems of the relations between the West and non-West, we cannot help asking what *is* the West, aside from the fact that it leads in the realm of production or productivity? Is the West, as many non-Westerners believe, to be defined simply by the fact that it produces a great deal and does it well? Thus this over-all view leads inevitably to conclusions—or to a varied but unique set of hypotheses—which form the basis for our discussions.

Before closing, I would merely like to suggest one or two possible conclusions, for there were none in my report, or rather they were phrased as questions. This was true primarily because this is the way I think—I mean I am an interrogative rather than a dogmatic person—and also because I assumed that questions should form the nucleus of our debates. What are these conclusions? There is one that some people read into my report, although it was not there. I refer to the extension, on a global scale, of the ideological abatement that we have seen taking place within Western societies. Although I did not express it, such a conclusion would be easy enough to draw from the way I stated the problem. In fact, this is the conclusion that Professor Rostow dared make in his analysis of the five stages. Western societies, having attained a certain level of both total and per capita production and having distributed the advantages of technical progress to the entire population, have provided an ever larger percentage of the population with decent living conditions. When this happens, ideological differences suddenly diminish, and it becomes clear that the problem of equality is no longer what it was in the past. Then it was a question of the equitable distribution of a certain fixed quantity of total wealth, whereas now it has become one of the decreasingly unfair distribution of a growing quantity of total wealth. After World War II, the West discovered that in our time any economic system distributes the benefits of technical progress to everyone, that the law of pauperization no more exists in the Soviet Union than it does in the West. Once having made such a discovery, there may still remain a certain number of differences—even meaningful differences—but it is conceivable that discussion can now become reasonable, if not rational, and no longer appear as a fight to the finish between ideologies.

This is not the conclusion I arrived at, for various reasons I would like to enumerate before I close. The first is that, taking the long view of things, we can obviously imagine the Chinese, Indian, and African worlds attaining a per capita level of production a few centuries hence which will rival that of England or France, or even of the United States. We can then let the imagination run wild as to what this will mean once the quarrels of the initial stages of industrialization are finished a few centuries hence. But we know that in a certain number of underdeveloped countries industrialization is extremely difficult, that these countries were already overcrowded when they began to industrialize, whereas in the West the problem of overpopulation developed together with industrialization. We also know that many traditional cultures are far more poorly adapted to the rational attitude of the worker than is the culture of the West; and furthermore, we see that the differences in wealth between the developed and the underdeveloped countries is tending to increase rather than decrease. Each time I allow myself to be tempted by the optimistic vision of the whole world pacified in an English sort of way, I remember Lord Keynes's phrase: *In the long run we are all dead.* This is one possible perspective, but not one of the distant future.

There are also other reasons which cause me to tread very carefully. First of all, I think that there can be as many variations in the political or moral organizations of industrial societies as there were variations in the social organizations of ancient societies. We might just as easily claim, really, that in all the ancient, neolithic societies the economy was of the same type. This community of structure on the economic plane did not prevent an extraordinary diversity in the social realm. We could also state that from the time complex societies began until the seventeenth or eighteenth century, the kind of economic organization was the same, and yet this did not prevent an extraordinary variety of social organizations, each of which justified itself by its own notion of what society should be. In our time, however, we have an added problem: Man is so determined to reap the benefits of the industrial society that it is difficult to prevent a semireligious aura from surrounding the organizational methods of the society. And when semireligious beliefs become involved with organizational methods, we enter a period such as the one we are now going through, where in spite of the community of economic structure each society considers that its way is the only way, the absolute good. And when someone, such as my friend Kennan or I, tries to say: "There is no economic or political organization which is absolutely good, there are only differences of degree," we run the risk of being attacked by both sides, since in a certain sense each needs to believe in its own absolute validity in order to maintain its own coherence. When a certain conception of social organization has been the keystone of a whole social order, it is not easy to see it reduced to the level of "preferable," or of one possibility among many.

Finally, there is another reason why I would not dare draw any hasty conclusions; that is, even if we assume that industrial society such as we know it has generally spread throughout the world, we still have no clear picture as to what man, using this society as a point of departure, will do with his life, what he would like to do with his life. And there is nothing to suggest or prove that all men will have the same idea on the subject. It would therefore be strangely superficial to conclude that because industrial society exists throughout the world, mankind will be unified. For a unified mankind would presuppose that everyone were in complete agreement about the notion of human life, that is, it would presuppose a religious or at least a philosophical unification. For the moment, this is out of the question. A community of these industrial societies can lead to all sorts of unpredictable results. But in my opinion it would be practically impossible to state that it would go so far as to create a common religion or common philosophy. After all, industrial society is no more than the collection of means necessary to provide the majority of the people with decent material living conditions—just that, and not an end. Even if mankind is tending to standardize his means, a historical, spiritual, and social unity would presuppose something more: a common notion of what man is and what he aspires to. For the moment, I see no sign at all of this last unity.

POLANYI: I have doubts about the notion of industrial society. There is no sure proof that industrialization derives from certain ideas, certain currents of thought. It is not merely a question of an attitude taking hold in underdeveloped countries which aspire to join the industrial society. In Albania, for example, we clearly see that the advent of the industrial society was due to a revolution and a totalitarian system set up through occupation by a foreign power. In such cases, the relationship between the spread of industrial society and the desire to industrialize is nonexistent.

ARON: I shall add one word: to study our present situation from the point of view of industry or the ideas which have given birth to this society to my mind constitute two complementary ways of approaching the subject. It is obvious that each of us has a preference, but I don't believe this difference is terribly important.

SALIN: I think that the notion of "Industrial Society" can be accused of the same failing as Max Weber's notion of "charismatic leader," that is, using the same term to define completely heterogeneous realities. If we apply the same notion of "Industrial Society" to countries of advanced capitalism, where the industrial society evolved out of an order that was half feudal, half nascent capitalist, and to what is taking place in Russia and China, the concept of society is reduced to its purely technical aspects. Industrial society, as Raymond Aron conceives of it, harks back not only to Comte but to Saint-Simon, Turgot, and even back to Joachim de Flore. It is merely a positivist transformation of de Flore's notion of the three reigns. Even if Mr. Aron refuses to be classified as a positivist, Turgot and Comte were still right in emphasizing that if you consider things in this light, the result is a conversion from the theological-metaphysical to the positive. Even if we go back to the roots of the idea, the concept of inevitability, which for Saint-Simon as well as Marx was essential, soon becomes self-evident, whether we like it or not. Now, everyone agrees that modern technology brings about social changes. But the critical question is whether or not the technical organization results in the technical-philosophical rearrangement of society which alone will give rise to the industrial society. Mr. Aron seems a prisoner of Colin Clark's viewpoint, which reduces economics to a matter of statistics and so prevents it from posing the really basic questions. Today these questions are no longer concerned with the conflict between the national and the international, characteristic of the nineteenth century, but rather with the question of individual existence versus global existence. Today the crucial question is this: Is it still possible for a state, or for Europe, to lead an "individual" life by escaping from the "global life" of industrial society and at the same time by freeing itself from its political, social, and economic tentacles? In the light of this question it becomes necessary to reject the "appeasement" implicit in the notion of industrial society, to the extent that it purports to transcend the conflict between capitalism and socialism; mistaking a convergence of industrial forms for the convergence of the societies themselves, it skirts the problem of passing from one society (taken as a certain order of human relations) to another, it glosses over the differences between modern societies (comparable to those in the various feudal societies), and prevents us from understanding the efforts of a country such as India. Using the ancient rural community life as a basis, India is trying to incorporate this new industry in such a way that a new society will result, a society radically different from those of the United States, Russia, or China.

DEL CORRAL: Mr. Aron believes that "Industrial Society" is an abstract category which we can use to measure any society's state of evolution, and that it can be generally applied. It must be added, however, that it is a historical category which has appeared only in the history of the Western world.

The societies of antiquity or of the Middle Ages cannot be defined in terms of their economic characteristics. The same is not true, however, for European societies from the nineteenth century on, because we introduce into the notion of "Industrial Society" certain elements which are not purely economic and certain values which, while not economic, are dependent on economic values. For in industrial society, all values coexist, but in a hierarchy which assigns top priority to industrial and economic values. This secularization and concentration of values helps explain the lessening of ideological conflicts and at the same time enables us to discover the causes of economic development, such as the importance of religion as a contributing factor in the birth of capitalism.

This *élan* will only be temporary, and this standardization, this secularization of values which results in economic growth will one day enable all values to flower, all constraints to be forgotten, unless it ends in the apocalyptic destruction of mankind. These two possibilities underline both the grandeur and the misery of our destiny.

IYER: Throughout this seminar we shall constantly be talking about logical constructions such as Western society, Western values, Western man, Western morality, and so on—phrases repeatedly used in the various papers that have been issued to us—and these categories are as extravagant and opaque as similar myths about Eastern wisdom, Eastern values, Eastern man, and so on. But although these are logical constructions which stand up under analysis, we cannot approach reality except through our conceptual apparatus, and the fact that for centuries Europeans, and more recently Easterners, have allowed themselves these myths has largely conditioned and distorted their picture of reality. In other words, the people who will most readily agree with this idea of a single Europe, which has been presented by Mr. Aron, will be those people of the East who prefer to think of Europe in a single ideological image, and this goes back to the glass curtain between Europe and Asia which stems from the Greek view of Persia and continues right through history.

By a glass curtain I mean the refusal on both sides to recognize that there is a curtain; the further refusal to realize that even if you can see people on the other side of the curtain you can't sense and contact them.

The reason why I stress this is because there are many people today who would really like to reduce this glass curtain itself to some kind of new iron curtain, and this is true the deeper you go into China, the farther East you go. The essential point about this glass curtain is really the continued insistence on both sides on making unique claims on the basis of universal values, so that Easterners and Westerners alike believe that they uniquely respect the dignity and worth of the individual, that they are distinguished by the value they place on love and charity and the qualities of the heart.

ARON: Two sorts of objections have been raised to the way the problem was formulated. On the one hand, the objection by our Indian colleague, Mr. Iyer, and on the other those raised by my friend Salin. Mr. Iyer's objections were aimed essentially at the way I used, or he thought I used in my speech or in my extemporaneous remarks, the terms "West" and "Europe" and the unification implicit in both words. And yet I don't for a moment believe that the West is a harmonious, absolute unity any more than is the Orient or the Soviet world. The fact remains, however, that the method of organizing work and the rationalization due to science which all mankind wants to adopt, did begin in specific societies that we can generally categorize as European or Western. When we report this fact, and when we talk about the non-West westernizing itself, we are merely stating an incontestable historical fact, one that is quite objective and in no way implies any superiority on the part of the West or suggests that their work methods have been discovered for the welfare of all mankind. It is possible that it will lead to an apocalyptic catastrophe. But when I posed the problem the way I did, I do not believe there was any value judgment implied.

As for the objection raised by my friend Salin concerning the use we make of the concept of industrial society, the discussion or the objections may be of several kinds. The primary objection may be one of vocabulary, that is, we may prefer another term—technical or scientific society, or rational society—and reasons may be advanced as to why these are as objectionable as the term I used. The problem is to ascertain that we're all talking about the same phenomenon.

The second objection had to do with the implications of the concept. He accepted the fact that there are certain features of work organization which are applicable on a world scale and which are in fact spreading throughout the world. But he refused to accept the fact that these features of the organization of work can be separated from the social, intellectual, and human context. I do not really believe there is a contradiction. There would be a contradiction if, when I posed the problem, I had implied that the elements were separable. I have never believed that the use of the Aristotelian concept of category, which then allows the study of species, results in the species being mixed up. To my mind, it is impossible to say that someone who takes note of the similarities of industrial organization between the Soviet and American societies is denying the extent of the differences in the areas of politics and ideology. There is no trace of "appeasement" in pointing out that there are common features, for points in common have never eliminated ideological differences.

I should also like to add one final remark on this subject.

Salin mentioned that the feudal systems were very different, but for him to be able to speak of the different feudal systems he had to utilize the notion of feudalism. To use the concept of feudalism is doing nothing more than using the method of a generic concept, which does not exclude specific variations. One final point: the question of inevitability which he thought he had detected in the way I stated the problem. Actually, there was no idea of inevitability, but if I were to answer by psychoanalyzing him, I would say to him that he wanted *not* to see the indispensable element which I did imply—indispensable as opposed to inevitable. By that I mean that I do not believe that within a given time all human societies will be industrialized like the United States. In the first place, who am I to say? And besides, there are many other possibilities—an atomic holocaust, for one. I do believe, on the other hand, that many human groups will be unable to adapt to this kind of society and will disappear, as many other human societies have disappeared throughout history. In this sense, I do not in the least believe in the inevitability of one vast human unit cast in an American- or Soviet-style society. I do believe, however—and I suspect this is why he reproached me—that is it indispensable for the societies which want to survive to borrow the scientific apparatus of work organization. I do not mean that growth is an end in itself, but to my mind it is an essential means for those societies intent on surviving; it is indispensable to keep living standards from falling as the population increases and it is imperative for the better developed societies to keep their economic systems moving ahead. In any event, I want it understood that I am not linking in my own mind the two adjectives that Auguste Comte always equated—indispensable and inevitable. Perhaps my friend Salin will admit that on this point I moved a slight step beyond the positivists by not mistaking indispensable for inevitable. In this sense, I feel myself as far as possible from positivism as from Marxism, for if the way the problem was stated might recall one or the other, the answer I gave is diametrically opposed. Both Comte and Marx used to say that, given a certain type of economy, a certain type of society, politics, and way of thought will follow. I say exactly the contrary: given a certain type of economic organization, the possibility remains open for various political regimes, various beliefs, various religions, and in the most profound sense of the term, various human communities. The dissociation between indispensable and inevitable is, in my opinion, the most clear-cut break between our way of thinking and that of a century ago, for the optimism of the past century derived from the belief that societies always did what they had to, whereas we now know that they often do the opposite of what they should. Thus I feel that my proposal was open, and not dogmatic.

Part I

The West and the Problems of the
U.S.S.R. and the Underdeveloped Countries

CHAPTER I: THE EVOLUTION
OF THE U.S.S.R.

SECTION A—THE POLITICAL EVOLUTION

KENNAN: Aron poses, first of all, the question as to the true aims of Soviet power. "Is the goal of Soviet policy," he asks, "the welfare of the individual, and is its totalitarian character to be regarded only as a means to the rapid achievement of this end? Or has the totalitarianism become an end in itself, so that the ultimate aim is merely," as he put it, "to bring about total tyranny in the name of abundance and liberation?"

I doubt that we can usefully pose this question so sharply, or invite so clean and tidy an answer. Russia is a country of contradictions; and the history of Soviet power is one long record of the confusion of ends and means.

When the Russian Revolution occurred, Russia already was, and had been for some three or four decades, in a process of quite rapid evolution away from the archaic political and social institutions of czardom, in the direction of the modern liberal state. The development of a firm judicial system was far advanced; a beginning had been made toward the development of local self-government; public opinion was becoming a force to be reckoned with.

There is no reason to doubt that this represented the natural and underlying trend of Russian society in this century—a movement occurring somewhat later in time than, but otherwise not dissimilar from, comparable movements in other Western countries—a normal response, actually, to the introduction of popular education and to other stimuli of the modern age.

While this long-term trend of Russian society was interrupted by the Revolution and its consequences, I can see no reason to doubt that it still represents the direction in which, over the long run, Russia must move.

Despite Lenin's intolerant temperament and the doctrinaire authoritarianism with which he governed his own party, there can, I think, be no question of the fundamental idealism of his purpose at the time of the Revolution. It was certainly with reluctance and with heaviness of heart that he was obliged to concede, initially, the necessity of the terror.

One can argue that terror is the inevitable outcome of any attempt to put a utopian vision into practice by the use of political authority; and with this, I would agree. But I doubt that Lenin was himself aware of this.

The Bolshevik movement was betrayed into terrorism and brutality by the strange sequence of events which carried it suddenly into power, contrary to its own expectations, in a single country where its active popular support was minimal, and where even the class it professed to represent—the proletariat—was only a tiny minority among the working masses. It was from this predicament that the early Bolsheviki hoped to be rescued by a general European revolution—and were not. They then found themselves confronted with the choice of resorting to terror or resigning what they believed was their natural and appointed place in history. Having no religious scruples that could have warned them against placing the ends before the means, they chose the terror.

Now the instruments of coercion, once created, have a tendency to find their own natural master. In Russia's case this was, of course, Stalin. It was with him that brutality was made into an end in itself. It was he who introduced the characteristic distortions of modern totalitarianism—the punishment of people not for the things they had done but for the things they might be presumed capable of doing; the substitution of blackmail for justice; the elevation of denunciation to the status of the highest civic duty; the cultivation of the anonymity and mystery and unpredictability of the punishing power; the creation of an artificial hell in the form of the forced labor and concentration camps; the reduction of the population, in short, to a state of general dread and mutual distrust.

It is idle to ask whether, for Stalin, happy prospects loomed at the end of this monstrous process of degradation. It was the only way he knew to protect his personal position and the integrity of his rule. Among a portion of the officials of Party and police, it came to be taken as the normal way of government.

To the people at large, however, to the intelligentsia above all, and even to a considerable portion of the Party, it was not only hateful but a source of shame and humiliation vis-à-vis the outside world, particularly the foreign socialist parties. Among those who took this position, Khrushchev occupied a prominent place, but he was by no means alone in this feeling, even within the Presidium of the Party. Most of his senior colleagues were prepared to concede that a large portion of Stalin's methodology was unhealthy and undesirable, though they often differed over the question as to how much of Stalinism ought to be discarded and how much to be retained.

What we now see in the Soviet Union represents a compromise among these differing views; the liberalization has scarcely gone as far as some would have liked to see it go. Nevertheless, it has gone so far as to represent a highly significant departure from Stalinism and an essential alteration of the nature of the regime. The regime has, to be sure, not barred itself in any legal or constitutional way from resuming former practices; it simply does not apply them.

But the aversion to these practices is still strong in the older generation; and a younger generation is growing up which is habituated to a greater freedom and to greater expectations of personal comfort than they could have dreamed of some years ago. It would be extremely difficult, today, to turn the clock back.

A distinction must of course be made here—and it is one highly relevant to Aron's question—between the system prevailing in the Soviet Union proper and that prevailing in outlying parts of the Soviet empire. We must recognize that in certain of these regions, notably East Germany, Czechoslovakia, and Hungary, the movement away from Stalinism has been not nearly so marked as in the Soviet Union itself. And we must ask ourselves: does this greater totalitarianism of the periphery of Soviet power represent a deliberate policy? Is it a condition which the Soviet leaders have deliberately cultivated, and are yearning to impose elsewhere? Or is it a response, involuntary and perhaps reluctant, to external necessities?

Here, too, the pattern is confused. There are still Stalinists in Moscow who would no doubt find quite normal the manner in which East Germany is now governed, and would be happy to see the same principles applied elsewhere.

But it is also clear that this view has not always prevailed. There are significant variations within the satellite area itself.

The regions where Stalinist controls are most firmly maintained are those which are most neuralgic from the standpoint of the cold war. The Soviet government, significantly, has not found it necessary to impose the Stalinist pattern on Finland, although that country has been for fifteen years fully and helplessly exposed to the full force of Soviet power.

We note, too, that where a local communist regime has had the courage, as in Poland, to repudiate of its own accord the excesses of Stalinist police terror, and to persist stoutly in this repudiation, Moscow has not seriously interfered. The crucial limit of Russian patience, to judge from the Hungarian experience, relates less to the extent of internal liberalization in a satellite country—provided, of course, the formal devotion to socialist principle is maintained—than to the degree of fidelity to the international security arrangements of which Moscow is the center. Had the Nagy regime not moved, in 1956, to denounce the Warsaw Pact, in circumstances which gave the Russians no assurance whatsoever that Hungary, if permitted to take this step, would not end up by joining the Atlantic Pact instead, it is not at all certain that the final Soviet intervention would ever have occurred.

If we weigh these various circumstances, we see that where strongly totalitarian features of government have endured the communist orbit, this has been for reasons having to do partly with the peculiarities of the local situation, or, in even greater part, with the pressures and necessities of the cold war.

In neither case would the controlling factor appear to have been any such thing as a disposition on the part of the Soviet leadership to inflict these totalitarian devices for their own sake.

The picture, I reiterate, is not a simple one. On countless occasions, when I have been asked which of two seemingly contradictory and incompatible realities is true in the Soviet Union, I have been obliged to say: both. This, too, is one of these instances.

There are still Stalinists in the Soviet Union—people who, from habit, from fear, or from limitation of vision, can think in no terms other than those of absolute domination, and for whom the utopian end product of socialism has become indistinguishable from a state of total political slavery.

But these are only a portion of the leadership. They do not command the confidence of the oncoming student generation. Their views are not the ones that have prevailed in recent years. From the long-term and short-term standpoints they would appear to be on the side of the waning, not the waxing, trends of Russian life.

In the main, the goals and trends of Russian communism lie along the same path as those of Western liberal-industrialism.

What divides the two worlds is not a difference in aim—what divides them is fear, timidity, the unsolved problem of eastern Europe, and the unhappy dynamics of a weapons race so absorbing that both sides tend to forget the issues of its origin.

TALMON: There can be no doubt but that the increasing liberalization in Russia constitutes an important milestone in the

history of the twentieth century, and even in the history of the
world. Several reasons can be advanced in explanation, all of
which may be true or all false. One already given is this: the
Soviets have triumphed, they are solidly entrenched, and no
longer have to resort to terror. Another possibility is the fate of
every belief and every fanatic ideology; in the long run a relaxation and adjustment does occur, for such is the nature of things
that tension cannot be maintained over a long period of time. It
is also possible that the large number of intellectuals, technicians,
and functionaries formed since the industrial revolution—and
because of that revolution—simply reject this form of terrorism
and despotism which reigned in the past. But there is another
reason which, curiously enough, has not been mentioned. In
my opinion, the growing liberalization in the Soviet Union can
be explained not so much by the industrial society as by the
fear of this society. I mean that this liberalization and lessening
of ideological tension represents a concern about the bomb by
the instinct of self-preservation. Although people may not consciously make this parallel, it is nonetheless true that they are
obeying the instinct of self-preservation.

As a matter of fact, I believe there is an important analogy
between the situation today and that of Europe at the end of
the seventeenth and beginning of the eighteenth centuries. At
the end of the Thirty Years' War and the Puritan revolution, the
spirit of tolerance triumphed progressively and we witnessed a
marked upsurge of interest in the sciences. This movement was
accompanied by a lessening of religious tension, a decline of
faith, and the spread of atheism and other forms of disbelief.
What were the reasons for it? Was it the fact that people had
suddenly discovered that science refutes religion's truth? Or that
science had opened their eyes? Their eyes had obviously been
open prior to the rise of science, but they had not been receptive
to or ready for it.

The truth is that as the wars of religion dragged to a close,
Europeans of both camps realized that this thirty-year war was
going to turn Europe into a pile of ruins and lead to the de-

struction of both rival parties. The combatants grew weary and their enthusiasm for mutual destruction rapidly waned. On the other hand, an interest in science flowered, and people were soon caught up in the thrill of new discoveries, scientific progress —anything involving science. I wonder if the enthusiasm in Russia over the sputniks and space flights does not constitute an antidote, a means of lowering tension, eliminating the underlying causes of the ideological war, and creating a new atmosphere which, to my mind, is far removed from the dialectic of the Bolshevik regime as such.

ARON: I agree with Mr. Kennan that the danger is not in a planned economy itself. I do not share my friend Hayek's opinion that any interference by the state is the beginning of enslavement. We have no example of totalitarianism evolving out of dirigisme in a democratic country. What does seem to me important—not so much in the planning as in the one-party system—is the ideological basis, the attempt by a sect—a minority—to impose on the rest of its compatriots, or on the entire world, a certain set of institutions. When Mr. Kennan says that after all a one-party system may not be all that bad, since we're not particularly fond of a multiparty system such as—to take an extreme example—the French have, I cannot accept this as a satisfactory reply. The main point is not a single party or several parties, and I would agree that there are many intermediate possibilities between Stalinist totalitarianism and the Western parliamentary system. The key is not authoritarianism or democracy; the key to our contemporary world is: can or cannot a single party, with monopolistic control of the ideology and ideological support, exist? The basic difference between Professor Postan and me on the one hand and you on the other is that you seem to imply that the single, ideologically oriented party in the Soviet Union might disappear. I am not so sure. Recently, at a congress of sociologists, I talked with several young Russian philosophers and sociologists. They are certainly better than their elders, and not dumb. You can talk with them.

But when you come down to brass tacks, when you tell them, "You are a privileged class, you have a one-party system but refuse to admit it; you deny your existence as a privileged class," they refuse to listen. They want to believe they are the proletariat and they are fulfilling a world mission by destroying the so-called capitalist enslavement. So they are still very much a prey to the ideological mentality. I'm afraid that this is one of the most pressing problems of our discussion.

A MEMBER OF THE AUDIENCE: As for the points on which Mr. Aron and Mr. Kennan disagree, I side with the former. While Professor Aron was careful to list the points which separate the culture and industrial system of the West from those of the Soviet Union, I have a slight suspicion that Mr. Kennan overlooked or concealed these differences from us. Now, we are here to venture a diagnosis and formulate the strategy our diagnosis calls for: it is therefore perhaps even more dangerous to camouflage these differences than to stress them for the purposes of our discussion.

On this subject, I disagree on three points which are relatively minor but which should be borne in mind.

The first is this insistence on discovering radical changes in Russia which are supposed to have resulted from the return to the liberal inspiration of the Russian Revolution. I do not share Mr. Kennan's optimism, for two reasons: first of all, I do not believe that Tchaadayev's liberal, humanitarian tradition is the only one behind the Russian Revolution. There is another— which the Russians know very well—which consists of carrying faith to its extreme—even to the point of personal mutilation. The Russians have an untranslatable word for this—*Izuviere*. It was this tradition Dostoevski had in mind when he wrote *The Possessed*. It occurs throughout Russian history and throughout the revolutionary movement. It played an important part not only as a source of inspiration for the Communist Revolution, but also in recruiting members for the Communist party, which was thought of as a group of people chosen for their emotional and moral affinity, in keeping with this particular tradition in Russian history.

As for the humanitarian or, if you prefer, Christian, aspect— I use Christian in the Western sense of the term—of course it exists with the Russians. We all know that most Russians did not associate themselves—at least wholeheartedly—with the fanatic *Izuviere* aspect of the Communist party. If they had, there would have been no need for a dictatorship, since the ultimate goal of any dictatorship is to impose the beliefs and ethics of a minority upon the majority.

I believe that on certain points the Russians have failed, and I also believe that Khrushchev's reforms are not the result of his having been "converted" or, as it has been claimed, of his "success"; the simple fact is that they have really suffered serious setbacks in two or three areas. They have not succeeded in winning over their youth, the universities, and they had to make some concessions. They realized that weakness results from certain excesses of dictatorship. This is why, if things continue to evolve in the same way, we may, during the next few years, see this liberalism spread and witness an increase in individual freedom and tolerance.

And yet, as long as the Party remains what it is—that is, a party whose aim is to impose an ideology and make sure its basic principles are not compromised—as long as this Party remains attached not only to Marxism as a historical concept but also to the idea of its historical mission to replace capitalism; and as long as everything we deem to be objective truths—law, justice, truth itself—are considered as instruments of the class struggle, or the means of replacing capitalism by communism, I do not think the basic differences between East and West will disappear.

The second point is somewhat difficult to explain. I would hazard the guess that sooner or later the liberalism of the nation will prevail over the fanaticism of the Party. The problem is, when? The Russians are actually exploiting every weakness of the Western world in order to replace our system by theirs. The question thus consists of trying to determine whether they will succeed before the era of tolerance and enlightenment begins.

The third point is that, in my opinion, it is dangerous to believe that the communist system is limited to Russia. To me, communism is an ecumenical phenomenon. Of course, it seems better to you in East Germany than in Russia, because there it lies on the periphery of Russia. And yet I feel it is worse there than in Russia itself because it is involved with and allied to the German's rigor, his sense of perfection, lack of subtlety, and perhaps a certain degree of innate brutality. I can of course imagine communism associated with all sorts of other cultural complexes which have nothing to do with this Russian tradition of liberalism; the Oriental despotism of China, for example. Chinese communism seems to me to be infinitely more menacing than Russian, not only because of the vast multitudes at its disposal, not only because the Chinese are prepared to go much further than the Russians have ever gone, but also because I have no idea what moral principles—principles which are foreign and hostile to us—serve as the basis for communist doctrine in China.

On one point I take issue with Mr. Aron—when he considers state planning to be fundamentally contradictory to liberalism. I do not of course go as far as Mr. Kennan, who declares that in certain areas planning should be one of the instruments of liberalism. What frightens me is the fact that certain countries embrace not a system of a planned economy, but the communist ideology concealed therein.

ROSTOW: With regard to the possible evolution of more "liberal" tendencies in the Soviet Union, which Mr. Kennan has discussed, I agree generally with what Professor Postan said. Of course there are strong currents at work in the Russian culture—currents which are profoundly changing the society inherited from the Stalin era. But it is too soon to say that such currents have prevailed, or even that they will. If we can reach a conclusion about these trends from what we have thus far seen, I should say—as both Mr. Kennan and Mr. Aron have remarked—that these developments foreshadow a system of law rather than one we could properly call a system of political democracy.

A highly developed and highly civilized system of law—one we could qualify as meeting the standards summed up in the popular expression, "The Rule of Law"—can exist, and has existed in nondemocratic societies. History offers many examples of the phenomenon. There is no necessary connection between political democracy and a legal system we can properly describe as meeting the criteria of the Rule of Law, a system which protects the individual against arbitrary action by the state. But we cannot stop with the distinction between democracy and the rule of law. It would be a play on the word "law" to suggest that two societies which have similar legal systems are for that reason identical, or are in the process of becoming identical. Of course, the considerable volume of legal literature produced behind the Iron Curtain—where real political and social freedom does not exist—exerts a significant influence on the minds of lawyers, judges, and professors of law in those countries. To be serious about the direction in which Soviet society is evolving, we should go further and examine a whole series of problems, of which I shall mention two or three as examples.

What level of individual liberty does the legal system afford? One can say that such differences are mere "differences of degree," but, as Holmes once remarked, all differences are really differences of degree—an observation of great insight. Thus I should start by inquiring whether the degree of freedom permitted the individual by the legal system is narrow or wide. Second, I should mention this question: what degree of strictness and rigor does the legal system require, when it seeks to avoid vague definitions of crime or tort, above all in dealing with crimes or torts of opinion? What is its definition of treason, and of all the forms of near-treason known to modern societies? Third, is the judicial power independent, and as strong as it is independent, and does it function as a strong and independent barrier against arbitrary action by the state or by private groups? For the guarantees written into the law are of no significance in themselves, unless they can be asserted and enforced by judges really free in relation to political authority and defended by lawyers who cannot be punished for having defended such rights in court.

Finally, I should suggest an even more fundamental issue which must be faced, in my judgment, before we accept optimistic views about the direction of development in the Soviet world. What minimum degree of individual liberty, protected by law, must exist before a society of law can hope to become a free society? Here we return to the range of issues which Mr. Aron and Professor Postan have just examined. I am not one of those who regard every intervention by the state into political or economic life as an immediate and positive threat to liberty. Nonetheless, I do believe that there can be no liberty to be protected by law in a society where the state has a complete monopoly of economic power, as the sole employer of all who work, and where the individual therefore has no real initiative in the conduct of his life. It follows that we should consider the problem of pluralism—the diffusion of authority among many centers of social power, that is to say, the existence of genuine alternatives among which the individual can choose, which can give real content to the idea of liberty—before we conclude that a genuinely socialist state can establish liberties capable of being defended by law.

KENNAN: If I were not convinced that the Communist party is actually in the throes of an internal crisis, I would not harbor the hopes I do concerning its evolution. I really think that what we are discussing boils down to the problem of the Party's future recruiting program; if the Party can enlist enough people whose ideas and opinions coincide with its own, then perhaps it can last for a very long time. But is this actually possible? You have to bear in mind the frame of mind of Soviet youth and the infiltration of antagonistic ideas into the Soviet Union. For Russia is now the center of an empire and, what is more, the younger generations of Russians are borne along on a wave of enthusiasm which demands to know what the rest of the world is thinking and talking about, and to obtain the permission to come in contact with these ideas.

On the other hand, what Mr. Rostow said about a legal system or a system of sovereign law is, in my opinion, extremely interesting, and I agree that the independence of the legal and judiciary systems is especially vital and apparently is nonexistent in Russia. And yet it seems to me that we can detect its appearance in the consciences of the Russian people—and this is in itself a promising start.

As for parliamentary institutions, I had no intention of stressing the point that in my opinion—and only in my opinion—they are absolutely essential to our way of life because of their constitutional role, that is, as a means of sanctioning constitutional rights and of changing governments. I also think that the possibility of changing a government by peaceful means alone is at the very basis of our democracy, and that nothing is more important.

A MEMBER OF THE AUDIENCE: I hope that Mr. Kennan's ideas will come to pass and that Soviet ideology will grow progressively more liberal, that is, that the sharp edges will be rounded and the differences between the Soviet system and ours will slowly diminish. We should not, however, exclude the possibility that the Soviet ideological system may take various, contradictory tacks; nor should we think that it will necessarily evolve constantly toward liberalism. I might remind Mr. Kennan that such a reversal has already occurred in the history of communist doctrine. The failure of the NEP economic policy was followed by a harsher, stricter, less tolerant period; in short, by a new wave of purity and extremism. It was then that Stalin, as if aware of what was going to happen, kept Trotsky from exploiting the economic situation for his own ends. As long as the education, propaganda, and the structure of ideas remain an arm of ideology, the possibility that intolerance and persecution may recur cannot be ruled out. I hope it never will. But we are discussing the details of strategy, and must be careful not to let ourselves be lulled into the childish attitude of waiting optimistically for events to happen as we would like them to.

KENNAN: I would like to clarify my thoughts on the question of how the Soviet regime will evolve and whether it may revert to Stalinism or, on the contrary, move in the opposite direction. Someone has expressed the opinion that the possibility of reverting to Stalinism, for instance, depended basically on the qualities and predilections of the man who, at a given moment, happened to be at the head of the Soviet system. I am of the opinion that this possibility depends just as much, if not more, on the nature and state of Soviet society itself and on the virtues of the members of the Party and of the new wave. This might offer interesting food for thought for a historian, but I think it would be worth while to remember in what conditions the Party found itself between the end of 1920 and the beginning of 1930. It was then vulnerable, ready to be taken over, exploited, and finally enslaved by a man of Stalin's ilk. After this period, new structures made their appearance in Soviet society. I am thinking particularly of what in the United States are generally called "interest groups"—captains of industry, officers, intellectuals, etc. Because these groups do exist, any attempt to impose on the Russia of today the totalitarian structure of the Stalinist era would pose an entirely different problem from that which existed from the beginning of 1920 to the end of 1930. This is one of the reasons why, in this area, I am more optimistic.

ARON: I personally do not believe a reversion to Stalinism is probable, and I agree with you that Soviet society is moving along the lines you suggested. But I also feel that two factors have to be taken into consideration: one is the fundamental nature of Soviet society; the other is the particular qualities of the person who happens to be in charge of it. Any leader of a political system has a profound influence on the way the system functions. And I might also say that even if a new premier were as nefarious as Stalin he could not operate in the same way Stalin did, because Soviet society has evolved. But he still might slow down, or stop for a generation, this evolution toward a more liberal society. I simply wanted to emphasize the fact that we should keep these two factors in mind.

KENNAN: Let me come back to certain points. First of all, to stress that for several years, that is, since the death of Stalin, a certain form of parliamentarianism has appeared. I admit it is extremely limited. The result is that Khrushchev's position and power are dependent upon the majority faction in the Central Committee. This became clear during the conflict with Molotov and Bulganin. After he lost the majority on the Presidium, Khrushchev found himself obliged to try to obtain a majority in the Central Committee. This seems to me a most interesting fact, for if we compare it to the evolution of British democracy, we note that we have a parliamentary system which issued not from the base but from the summit. Also, in the eighteenth century, not many people worried about parliamentarianism in Great Britain. This may well be an encouraging sign that we ought to bring out during our discussions.

The fundamental trait of a nontotalitarian society is that justice must not be completely arbitrary, and that people can rely on laws and courts of law. No one is arrested arbitrarily and imprisoned for political or any other reasons. But in the Soviet Union, the judiciary system, though it may not conform to our ideal, still does exist and is functioning.

As for the relationships, however unsatisfactory, between public opinion and the means employed to transmit power, they constitute the only way of avoiding a repetition of the bloody events which marked the early centuries of Russian history, and the acts of violence which accompanied the death of a czar and the advent of his successor. This weakness is still inherent in the Soviet government, and yet it may be less so as this new form of parliamentarianism spreads. It is probable that the progress already made is in the direction of our own institutions. They are still a long way from the curious, complex system of administration and elections operative in the United States. Nor do I believe that this system could be applied to other countries, not because the people are not "advanced" enough, but merely because they are quite different from what we are.

If it appeared to you I was predicting what would take place in Russia, then I expressed myself poorly. I wanted to point out that we are now a long way from Stalinism, and that this fact should be noted and borne in mind during these discussions. On the other hand, as far as Orwell is concerned, when *1984* first appeared I discussed it at great length with friends who, like myself, have spent considerable time in Russia. After a great deal of careful thought, we concluded that Orwell's nightmare is a fiction, that the totalitarian phenomenon is a temporary malady which strikes societies and which bears within it the seeds of its own destruction—not a sort of permanent enslavement which can be imposed upon mankind.

Finally, I would like to say that the precise distinctions made by Mr. Aron in his paper are worth while but that the problem posed does exist; it is not made up. It would, of course, be wonderful if the world we lived in were as simple, and everything as clear as that. I am not contending that Stalinism does not exist in the U.S.S.R.; it does, and the whole Party apparatus is in the hands of confirmed Stalinists such as Suslov. One entire wing of the Soviet regime is strongly, almost unremittingly Stalinist. But I maintain that this official government, this official "line" is being seriously questioned by certain elements of Soviet society, principally the intellectuals and the youth. I think it is of the utmost importance for us to recognize this fact; otherwise we are committing the error of a good number of my compatriots who refuse to see any difference whatsoever between 1949 and 1959, and thus are very pessimistic about the possibilities of avoiding a nuclear war.

It would be tragic for us to go on judging in terms of pure Stalinism—because it is easier to do so—and ignore the subtleties or ambiguities of the Soviet situation. This would only lead us down the road to terror and despair.

SARTORI: We ought not to be optimistic about long-term political problems. Listening to Mr. Kennan, I had the feeling—and I think he'll forgive me if I err in trying to interpret what I heard—that he believes in the natural course of history, as others believe in the laws of nature. The impression I got from his talk is that the two worlds in question are converging, that the differences between them will diminish as time goes on, and that, human nature being the same everywhere, in the long run Russia will be very much like Europe; that even their institutions will become similar and a new parliamentarianism will make its appearance. I was struck by this last remark, as I was also struck by another he made, namely, that the defective two-party system which he believes to be that of the United States is not so different from the one-party system which, as he sees it, corresponds to a pseudo-bipartisan type. I'm afraid I cannot accept this viewpoint, which underestimates certain fundamental aspects of our own system and on the other hand overestimates certain minor aspects in the current evolution of the Soviet situation. In other words, I gather that Mr. Kennan is not evoking what I call the "Orwellian" possibility. And yet the other possibility—that reason and human nature will overcome the temporary obstacles—has been mentioned. Before I conclude I would like to come to the defense of Orwell. Obviously I don't want to see his predictions come true, but I want to emphasize that they still may, and nothing we have seen till now has convinced me otherwise.

ARON: I would add only one word. I think in this case it would be a good idea to make a clear-cut distinction between the internal evolution of Soviet society and the possibilities of war or peace. It is not clear in my own mind that the relatively liberal Russian society will cease to be the enemy of the United States; in fact I can conceive of peace being maintained between the United States and the U.S.S.R. on the sole basis of reason or, if I may say it, the completely irrational nature of war. The two questions should therefore be treated separately. But it is obvious that it will be easier for us to coexist with a "liberal" than with a Stalinist Russia.

SECTION B—THE ECONOMIC EVOLUTION

The Theory of Conspicuous Production

POLANYI: The ideas I would like to set forth for you are still in an unfinished form, although they represent the fruit of long reflection. First, let me briefly recall how they came about, since they were the subject of violent controversy. The main fact which concerns us is the decision taken in 1920 by the Soviets to establish a totally planned economic system. The decision was made on ideological grounds; I also believe that the way the system was applied was based on ideological considerations: to establish an entirely new basis for human relations. This was to be accomplished by abolishing private ownership of the means of production and ceasing the manufacture of consumer goods. The elaboration of this economic system was predicated on the hypothesis that the nationalization of industry, that is, the establishment of legal control, would result in an effective takeover by the central administration. In the opinion of the central authority, this over-all plan would have the support of the masses, given the nature of the power—actually emanating from the proletariat—charged with preparing and getting it started. This plan consequently promises, or did promise, to replace a self-seeking, disorganized, and chaotic system of production with a scientific and brotherly co-operative system.

These promises, which I think were illusory, were part and parcel of the Bolshevik ideology. The plans drawn up by the Soviets were aimed at satisfying the moral passions on which this ideology was based. As early as 1920 certain voices were immediately raised (especially that of Ludwig von Mises) declaring that central economic direction was impossible, because the alternate choices had to be guided by the market. Today I believe that this argument was basically sound, although it left some unanswered questions. In short, its main weakness was that it went too far in stating that public ownership could not work because it excluded the use of market relations among industries. This theory was implicitly abandoned when, after a period of extreme hardship, it seemed that the Soviet system of public ownership was working and producing satisfactory results. In 1936, F. H. Knight offered a new slant to this argument: he declared that a centrally controlled, planned economy can only be created at the price of a complete suppression of liberty. In other words, planning is not impossible, it is immoral, evil; it opens the "path to enslavement."

At this point, I have to go back to an idea I first formulated a decade ago when I disputed the soundness of this theory and offered a modified version of Mises' theory. Basing my argument on general principles which limit the possibilities of administration, I noted that this control was so restricted that it was impossible, even when it was legally invested in the central authority, to exercise it effectively; thus the higher echelons were incapable of carrying out certain operations, especially those dependent on the mutual adjustment of all the basic units which are subject to control. The market was conceived in terms of one of the possibilities of mutual adjustment and within the favorable framework of these adjustments. But no network of mutual adjustments among a multitude of centers can be created by a hierarchical organization relaying its orders to these centers. This is especially true of a network of market relations. The number of relations this network regulates per unit of time exceeds by several million the number of relations that can be regulated by a superior hierarchical authority.* At that time, I explicitly accepted the possibility that nationalized industries might be managed in accordance with market relations, and in fact concluded that they should be so managed, within the framework of over-all planning, about which I shall have more to say in a moment. This idea, which found no acceptance ten years ago, is today accepted in many countries—although I have never received any credit for it.

On the other hand, I had also reached another conclusion—which even today is not extremely obvious—that will serve as my point of departure: if the Soviet economy is functioning more or less satisfactorily, it is because it is in reality a "camouflaged market economy." In my opinion, market operations take place outside the system of general direction, and I might even go so far as to say that the violence to which the central system has been subjected is in large part meant to give the impression that it is a centrally controlled system, and to make the people think that the government is adhering to its ideological principles. Certain signs would seem to confirm this impression; I shall enumerate them, since they will shortly help buttress my theory.

First, the commercial aspects—especially money and profit—which after numerous excuses the government introduced, even though they are in conflict, or even incompatible, with the ideological aspirations of the government. Second, technology is used under the same conditions as in the West. We should bear in mind—for it is sometimes overlooked—that technology is not a physical but an economic conception which, through the transformation of products, enables us to assign them a plus value. The relative evaluation of means and ends depends on what system of economic comparison is used. Actually, the same technical names are used for the same techniques both under the Soviet system and under our own Western system. Third, a curious feature of central planning which I had pointed

* The proof of this thesis may be found in my book *Logic of Liberty* (London, 1951).

out several years ago—the over-applause given to the results obtained obviously shows that there is no real desire to co-ordinate the different elements of the plan. If there were, those areas which exceed their quotas would be considered as much a failure as those where quotas have not been met; and yet the Soviet system tends to offset underfulfillments by overful-fillments. Fourth, various studies and reports have revealed interindustry transactions of an illegal nature, suggesting that they play an important role in meeting the quotas. Last, there is proof that this plan actually derives from the initiatives of enterprises on a local level and is the fruit of their suggestions. If this is so, then we are dealing with an agglomeration of plans and not with a plan in the real sense of the term—an originally conceived master plan. This distinction will become clearer later on in my report.

I obviously must admit that in case the systematic camou-flaging of a market does exist, it plays a role which modifies the economic life and reduces the efficiency which would obtain in a really free market. This is why I maintain that the Soviet sys-tem of over-all planning has functioned rationally only to the extent that it has operated through a network of market rela-tions, even though they may be camouflaged and polarized by an artificial hierarchy of central planning.

We shall come back to this point in a moment. Meanwhile, I shall discuss another theory which will also help us clarify our thinking. As you know, the shortcomings of the market principle have been increasingly demonstrated over the past decade or two. The market system is notably blamed because the market cannot balance collective demands. It is incapable of deciding whether priority should be given to the construction of a network of highways or a system of high schools. It can-not balance social costs, nor can it correct imperfect competi-tion, monopolies, or oligopolies. It cannot evaluate or regulate the list prices of newly developed industries or public works. Finally, it cannot control effective demand, at least in the sense that Keynes—whose theory I subscribe to—understood it.

These operations or functions should therefore be carried out, insofar as it is possible and even if it is done imperfectly, by the public authorities. By so doing, public authorities serve to regulate, guide, and supplement market tendencies. This function, which is now generally known as "over-all planning," enables the market tendencies which do appear to be utilized, but not suppressed. I shall use the term "market" solely in the sense of "over-all planning" within which the market operates, and so avoid having to repeat the definition.

This definition will serve as the point of departure for today's discussion. This position which I had adopted now seems to me subject to two major objections, the first of which I discovered in a book by the Hungarian economist, Janos Kornai.* This book has led me to admit that in a system of over-all planning such as we have seen in Hungary for many years, management is not essentially concerned with the question of profits, for although this aspect cannot be totally neglected, it is not the cornerstone of production. In fact, contrary to what I had thought, management is guided by directives or detailed instructions which emphasize bonuses—job bonuses—rather than profits. This system does not seem to allow effective scope for the operation of market relations. This is the objection that Peter Wiles has raised concerning my views; it has not been given serious enough attention.

The second reason which led me to revise my position is perhaps even more important. If it is true that the Soviet system is a camouflaged market economy subject to numerous distortions, then we should agree that it must be extremely inefficient, given the top-heavy bureaucracy. Yet all indications suggest that its level of productivity is high, higher even than market economies where there is full employment.

This is indeed strange. Could it be that the supposed distortions of the market actually favor productivity? If so, in what way? This mystery was noted and discussed for the first time by

* Janos Kornai, *Overcentralisation in Economic Administration* (Oxford University Press, 1959).

one of the most distinguished specialists of Soviet economy, who wrote:

"The elements of inefficiency are so striking that they may create the impression that Soviet industry is grossly ineffectual and scarcely to be taken seriously. Such an impression would fly in the face of all we know about Soviet industrial performance." *

This contradiction must be taken seriously, and herein lies the mystery. The same curious fact is also mentioned in Kornai's book. The entire work is an inventory of the shortcomings of the economic system, shortcomings which the author considers inevitable. I shall have more to say about that in a moment. These lacunae are all identified and condemned by comparison with a capitalistic market. Although this system is implicitly considered much inferior to market operations, Kornai nowhere rejects it, but neither does he advocate a Yugoslav-type market.

Kornai shows that there is a connection between the dynamic quality of the system and its inefficiency, that is, between two factors which can neutralize each other. He recalls the pride with which Stalin used to say: "In the Soviet Union, the consumption of the masses, that is, their buying power, is constantly growing; by outstripping the growth of production, it stimulates production." Kornai's answer is that the increase in buying power may encourage the planners but it does not incite the enterprises to do better work; rather it induces laziness, negligence, and the disregard of the buyers' needs. But why does it stimulate the planners? Here we put our finger on the crux of the mystery.

Fortunately, it is possible for us to study a similar situation—though it is on a much smaller scale, I agree—that of the United Kingdom in 1947. At that time, *The Manchester Guardian* published an excellent study of industry in the United Kingdom which showed that the factories were working to full capacity, and even beyond capacity, since production sometimes had to

* Berliner, *Factory and Manager in the U.S.S.R.* (Harvard University Press, 1957), p. 326.

be halted because of a shortage of raw materials or a dearth of manpower. Deliveries were inevitably late, the choice was considerably reduced both as to date of delivery and the quality of the goods delivered. During this sellers' market, when, as Sir Stafford Cripps put it, "too much money was in pursuit of too few goods," the economy was dynamic and booming, even though work stoppages did occur, the quality of merchandise was sometimes poor, and deliveries were capricious.

I should like to interject a note of economic theory, using a truism which is not often enough taken into account as my point of departure. Physical products, which are generally called goods merely by virtue of their bodily existence, actually are not; they are merely potential goods, whose real value depends on their relation with the recipient. To evaluate a list of goods at our own prices and the prices normally prevailing in our own market is to assume that these goods are delivered to their recipients as aptly as goods are normally delivered in a normal market. I shall call this "their normal market value." Yet the value of products delivered irregularly and destined for less discriminating buyers should in fact have a lower value. I shall call this their "actual value" in a sellers' market. Thus the value of a series of products depends on the way it is distributed, and in a sellers' market the same products have a lower actual value than they do in a normal market. I do not believe this point has been studied as theory and I therefore have no compunction about stating that I am about to introduce a new point of theoretical study.

At this juncture, I should like to emphasize a special form of diminishing value in a sellers' market. The more limited the variety of products, the more restricted the consumers' choices. As a result, it is impossible to assign an exact value to an article or group of articles taken by themselves, independently of the assortment to which they belong. In other words, the value of an object increases according to the variety of the assortment to which it belongs. A predominantly sellers' market will tend to reduce the assortment, or at least keep it from increasing.

Consequently, merchandise produced under these conditions will be overvalued by comparison with prices prevailing in a normal assortment. To my knowledge, statisticians have never taken into account the fact that an assortment has a different value from the sum of the articles it includes.

I should now like to describe in these terms a market favorable to sellers, because this description relates directly to the question I shall take up next: a production system based on targets. We are still dealing here with a sellers' market, and if we presuppose a normal situation of full employment—with, let us say, a figure of 3 per cent unemployed—we see that, as the effective demand increases, the total number of articles manufactured increases. This process may be accompanied by a per capita decrease in productivity in volume, and in all probability by a per capita decrease in value, that is, in customer satisfaction. The total value of production may even decline when the material volume increases. When I talk about this to my fellow economists, they say to me: "How can you measure that? You can't—so don't talk about it." First of all I refuse to accept the philosophical validity of such an objection, and second, I am prepared to go even further out on a limb and at least try to measure the kind of difference I'm referring to. It is not impossible to estimate the potential decrease in value in a sellers' market by comparing in our own market prices paid for merchandise from a good assortment with those paid for a less discriminating allocation, such as a meal from a fixed menu as compared to one chosen à la carte; or a series of clothes ordered in advance for delivery at specified intervals; or leaving on a trip and returning at specific dates; or the purchase of a uniform instead of a suit chosen from a normal assortment. From such examples, I estimate that the value generated by satisfying less discriminating consumers may be less than half the value of the same goods sold in a normal market.

My conclusion concerning a sellers' market is this: in such a market, we can detect the nascent characteristics of a system I shall call the system of conspicuous production. If the goal of industry is influenced by the desire for quantitative results which can be expressed statistically, production for a sellers' market can reach a level clearly superior to that for a normal market. Can you begin to see the outlines of what I would like to call a "para-economic system"? This is what I term a system of conspicuous production. Here there is actually a correlation between dynamism and scandal, whenever the statistical results increase at the expense of the economic value produced. As I have already suggested, under these conditions the value of the statistical results may be rated at more than twice what they would be according to our own normal evaluations, or if the goods were calculated in terms of the prices they would command as part of a normal assortment in a normal market.

If this were true, it would more than suffice to explain the whole history, if not the whole meaning, of "economic targets." In any event, I ask your indulgence to carry this a step further, because we may be able to cull certain useful concepts by discussing not only a sellers' market, but also a centrally controlled market. I shall term this "target production," and move from an analysis of a sellers' market to the theory of target production.

We should bear in mind that in the Soviet Union this sellers' market is very rigidly controlled. Prices are controlled and do not affect either profits or investments. There is no inflationary spiral in the usual sense of the term. Commercial considerations become less and less important. Production is not guided by profits, which are controlled and give only an approximate idea on which to base economic decisions. The situation is similar to that in which prices are controlled and goods rationed at the same time. Then various personal factors come into play when a merchant sells his goods, such as a friendly or inimical attitude toward his customers. In England, we could read the price fluctuations of cigarettes—which were rationed—on the faces of the tobacconists. As soon as the prices went down, the storekeepers' humor soured and they became impolite. Thus they derived a sort of consistent income out of discourtesy and so balanced supply and demand. Since they went on being impolite, demand declined to a level at which prices were adequate. This phenomenon is in fact absolutely general: depersonalized monetary relations are thus replaced by relations which are personal and specific.

This freedom of action can be transferred to a higher authority, who may exercise it by equating a sum of individual satisfactions with the image of a collective satisfaction. How does this factor come into play? Actually, it has to do with the ideological notion I have already mentioned. It comes into play because it is thought that the sum of individual satisfactions is a matter of public responsibility, and thus has a collective significance.

I believe this is a very important distinction, one that I tried to make some time ago when I first approached the problem by in fact suggesting that the whole notion of "economic targets" was irrational. It might appear reasonable to say that today England produced half a million tons of coal, but at the same time it could scarcely be deemed reasonable to say that today England shaved ten million chins or blew twenty million noses. There is obviously something false here, and we can show even more clearly why it is false to equate a sum of individual demands and individual gratifications with a collective satisfaction, by imagining a team of chess players. A team of chess players makes a certain number of moves, and we might say that during the next round the plan calls for the movement of sixty pawns, twenty knights, fifty bishops, and five rooks. This would obviously make no sense, and the example seems almost shocking. But if we in fact assume that the rules of the game could be so modified that neither of the players could lose, this game could be played with collective targets. A certain number of moves could be allocated to the pawns, etc., and nothing would happen. No one would lose, and the game would obviously lose all meaning. This rough example can teach us a good deal. It shows why an aggregate of individual plans is not a comprehensive plan. It is not because it does not succeed in grasping the underlying reasons which justify the individual plans. Individual plans can only be depicted as a whole, therefore, if their real significance is overlooked and they are considered merely as the physical act of pushing pieces on a chess board. A comprehensive plan of moves in a game of chess is logically admissible only if the rules of the game are so modified that neither player can win or lose. Applied to economic planning, this means that insofar as individual economic actions are not subject to the rules of profit (that is, by the effects of a sellers' market), they can be thought of and manipulated as the details of a collective work, but a work without meaning. On the other hand, to the degree that market prices still play a role, any collective economic plan is simply an aggregate of individual plans disguised as a collective work. Such a system functions rationally only to the extent that it includes and utilizes a whole series of market decisions.

Now let us go back to the point where I said I suspected that there was something false about this planned economy: first of all, that the very rules of technology imply a function of production by which certain processes will increase the total value as it is evaluated by the market where the technique in question is utilized. In the second place, there is a system of prices. In principle these are inflexible, but I suspect they must nevertheless manage to approximate the elements of supply and demand; otherwise they would be useless, and the government would have to assign quotas without resorting to monetary payments and without introducing monetary needs into the economic cycle. We also note that in a directed economy the total values are calculated in terms of these prices and are largely used to calculate the grand total of production quotas. Therefore, there must be some equivalents for these prices.

If each enterprise were autonomous and could get along on its own raw materials, and if two preliminary conditions were always present—the technique of para-economic prices and an excessive over-all demand—we could easily arrive at a sort of para-economic production seemingly based on "physical targets." But in reality, enterprises have to rely on a common fund of resources and must also look to one another for their raw materials, machines, and semifinished products. They proceed to a mutual allocation of resources by means of a ramified network of supply and demand. How can this horizontal network be operated in such a way as to allow each enterprise to count on its suppliers and customers? How is this possible without a market? Obviously, this is a crucial point, but I believe the difficulty disappears when we examine Kornai's report more closely. You may recall that in 1920 the Soviets created a centrally controlled system for the allocation of resources. The attempt collapsed into complete paralysis, and the economy was promptly baptized "war communism" (a term Western writers passively accepted). Thus the crucial moment of our age, which witnessed the decisive defeat of socialism's cherished goals, has been completely forgotten both in the Soviet Union and abroad. From 1930 or 1931 on, no further attempt was made to allocate or distribute resources from the center, and all directives are based on the proven operations of an already existing network of supply and demand flowing between the enterprises before the directives are drawn up and issued. This concrete experience —what is actually happening and what the practical and proven results are—is the cornerstone of the so-called planning, that is, of the directives. And no directive is issued—this is the second very important point—more than three months in advance. Naturally, for these brief quarterly periods, only small increases in production—a few percentage points—are called for. A relatively few centers of production have to be included, but this presents no major problem. In any event, all the enterprises will be urged to increase their production constantly. Third, this pressure leads to some extremely uneven rates of expansion. Some targets are exceeded, others are not met, and the fact that these variations do exist—as Kornai's book amply demonstrates—is of major importance, for all the higher authorities are interested in is the average over-all increase. This leads us to the key of the following problem. How do the central directives emerge from a sum of local initiatives? Having duly noted the over- and underfulfillments of the various enterprises under their control, the higher authorities use them as their basis for establishing quotas for the following period. The economic target for the succeeding period is therefore equal to the results of the previous period to which is added a small coefficient of expansion. Here then is the central formula for this so-called over-all economic planning. It orders the center of an already existing para-economic network to increase its production by a few percentage points over the previous results, which in turn had been obtained in similar fashion, and so on back to the beginning of the system.

There is, of course, an over-all planning which controls the allocation of pressure for the entire economic system, but all the detailed directives are determined by local conditions as shown by the enterprises' latest report. Central direction here plays no greater role than in any kind of capitalist-type system of over-all planning. What we are dealing with here is a poly-centric mutual adjustment, which is not a commercial system although it comes close to it to the extent that its para-economic norms approximate true economic norms.

We now come to an especially interesting aspect of the question, which is the actual object of Kornai's work: a systematic study of the anomolies which result from what I call the para-economic nature of Soviet production. The central authority has to evaluate the results obtained by the various enterprises, using quantitative targets such as total production, per capita yield, quality—all of which must be measured objectively and separately, not in terms of how much they contributed to profitability. The fulfillment of these targets automatically means substantial rewards or premiums. This is how the system operates, according to its own nature, and it could not operate otherwise. One point, however: the fulfillment of quotas is an extremely deceptive criterion. Kornai's book is one long demonstration of the fact that it is not possible to define quantitative targets—that is, volumetric quotas combined with para-economic indices such as the method and system of Soviet prices—

without arriving at some scandalous results. These results are of two sorts. One, enterprises will inevitably use the margin of freedom which their obligation to meet targets allows them to gain premiums by methods the authorities had overlooked—we might call this the overacquisition of premiums—and these methods will frequently be uneconomic, wasteful, and absurd. If, on the other hand—and this is the second point—the higher authorities object to this tendency on the part of the enterprises and make the tests more stringent (which they are continually doing), these enterprises will too often be paralyzed, find it impossible to take the steps they should, and be compelled to renounce them. Kornai regards this situation as an internal contradiction of the system.

These last remarks take me back to what I have said about a sellers' market and lead me to apply it to the target system of production. Directives issued within the framework of this system aim to some extent at moving the center of economic activities away from buyer satisfaction, which is the focal point of a normal market, toward the fulfillment of targets defined in physical terms, and taking para-economic prices into account. The value of these products as measured in normal market prices will tend to be much higher than the value of the product in a rival economic system controlled by a normal market; but its real, adjusted value—taking into account the noneconomic aspect of a much less discriminating need satisfaction—will always be lower. Thus I submit that what I said about a sellers' market applies even more to a target system of production.

If in fact we determine the value of the list of manufactured products in our own prices, we arrive at an overevaluation which seems to suggest an extremely large output; but if we correct for the fact of a less discriminating satisfaction of needs, the total product will be less than that of a normal market. In this sense it is true to say that so-called over-all planning operates rationally only insofar as it simulates market relations. Yet, since its production statistics are higher, the society gains in ideological satisfaction what it loses in material satisfaction. We might perhaps describe this phenomenon as a "maximizing" of over-all satisfaction in a society for whom collective dynamism and prestige are worth the price of individual comfort.

Even so, this does not explain the difference between an openly commercial society and one which claims to be completely planned. The existence of a planned economy is an ideological myth, supported by a masquerade. It is a bit ironic that the antieconomic characteristics of this masquerade produce statistics which simulate a higher productivity than in the commercial system from which these antieconomic characteristics derive.

ARON: Until the final three minutes of Polanyi's paper, I kept wondering whether he was going to conclude that the systems were fundamentally different or basically the same. For his entire analysis leads to one of these two conclusions, depending on whether one applies the yardstick of sociology or economics. I need not remind you that the theory of conspicuous production is borrowed from, and is a variation on, Veblen's formula. Veblen had tried to use conspicuous production to define a certain social class of Western society. It is interesting that Polanyi went back to his formula to apply it to another system, for, sociologically speaking, we should compare spectacular consumption to spectacular production. Is an economic regime whose goal is to produce the maximum number of physical entities, which are not necessarily economic goods since they are not related to consumer desires (to produce the maximum quantity of goods regarded as physical quantities constitutes—sociologically—a certain type of economy), basically similar to an economy where consumer demand and taste are given top priority, or virtually top priority (although, sociologically, it is a different system)? The goods referred to by Polanyi are for the most part consumer goods, but their quality and type are more or less determined by the planners rather than the wishes of the consumers. Polanyi's contribution in the realm of theory is, I believe, to have demonstrated that our methods of calculation, that is, the comparison of growth rates and production, are theoretically tainted by the fact that we use our prices to estimate the total volume of goods produced, whereas if we took into account the discrepancy between the products and consumer requirements, we would be compelled to reduce considerably the economic value of this production. I believe this to be an important theoretical contribution; other economists, who are not followers of Polanyi, knew that the Soviet consumer was obliged to take what he was given, they knew there was no adaptation either in quality or timing, but they nonetheless ignored these factors in making their comparisons. What Polanyi has done—and this is his major contribution—is to show us an additional error in the comparison of total goods produced, for one system is based on realistic pricing, while the other is based on fixed prices in a fictitious economy.

BICANIC: It will be extremely difficult for me to comment on Polanyi's immensely provocative report in the short time accorded. First, I agree with him that there is a difference—frequently overlooked—between the word "planning" taken in the economic sense and the meaning given it by Soviet apologists not only in socialist countries, but also in other countries such as the United States. Last year I had a long discussion about the word "planning" with several American specialists of Soviet affairs, for whom the term applies only to one clearly defined type of centralized, authoritarian planning, such as is offered in stereotyped versions of the Soviet Union. I concur with Professor Polanyi that a distinction must be made between the real and the apparent or "norm-type" economy. But on this point I should like to know what Professor Polanyi means by "over-all planning." Obviously, over-all planning does not include every decision made by the planners, for these decisions are restricted to certain quantitative decisions, certain choices of product types and operational activities for those charged with carrying out the plan. The result is that, by its very definition, planning is limited, it is not "total" but more or less decentralized at various levels of action. One may well ask what in a plan is decentralized—the preparation of the plan, the decision making, or the application and control of the plan?

This raises the following question: what use is planning? This is the same as evaluating the rationality of planning and destroying the ideological Messianism which some people may feel in planning.

I might add that I am not a partisan of Mises' opinion, neither the 1920 nor the 1935 version. I think that once this limit is set, it is possible to plan. One may well wonder whether, after all, there really is a market economy or a wholly planned economy. On this point, I might mention an experience I had in Texas. Texas businessmen are all advocates of the free enterprise system. Yet if the railroad company, which controls oil production because it controls the oil pipelines, were to order the oil producers to operate on a seven-day month, they would acquiesce. If the order called for eight days, they would again comply, although the oil magnates are all for free enterprise. But if stable and sufficient profits can be obtained by distorting principles, no one is going to object. The important question is to ascertain whether planning is an overriding necessity of industrial society or whether it is a caprice, a fixation of some dictatorial leaders in given countries. I am with those who maintain that it is an innate necessity of a developed industrial society. For example, it is impossible to create a railroad system in a country unless the distance between rails is everywhere the same, unless there are timetables, a rate policy—all of which must be regulated. These conditions are not necessary for highway transportation, although it is interesting to note that in the United States bus transportation is beginning to assume a form of planning. I obviously have no quarrel with Professor Polanyi about the ideological aspect of planning. Otherwise, how would Lenin have managed to centralize the activities of tens, of hundreds of millions of men toward the pursuit of a single goal? But to what extent is this activity centralized and to what extent is it a psychological Messianism applied to economics? I shall try to offer some answers to these questions.

To what extent are the activities of millions of men centralized? Here it is especially interesting to recall Stalin's words, which Professor Polanyi quoted: in one case, the increase in the consumer's buying power inevitably exceeded the production of consumer goods. In other words, planning always contained an inflationary element which readjusted the plans. This is, moreover, an extremely important psychological measure, for it acts as a stimulant in the fulfillment—or overfulfillment—of the targets set by the plan. I realize that overfulfillment is a sign of poor planning, as is its opposite. But this is not the question. I wonder if the pressure about exceeding prescribed quotas does not imply that the managers of socialist enterprises have reached a tacit agreement to oppose the rules and draw up two plans— one for themselves and one for their experiments. This is in fact what happens in countries with a Soviet-type planning. There is a price system, as well as a system of incentives in the form of profits sharing (profits being defined by law and administrative rules). In a communist society, the rate of general profit is set in advance by the government and is divided from top to bottom by a system of averages, so that the true reports are distorted and it becomes impossible to ascertain what the rate of profit allocated to an individual enterprise actually corresponds to.

I would like to draw your attention to one or two other points. First, the sellers' market no longer constitutes the major pressure on planning in the Soviet Union; what is developing is a buyers' market. In my opinion, the changes that have recently taken place in the Soviet economy—as well as the liberalization of the economy—are due to this gradual movement from a sellers' to a buyers' market. A few years ago, the expression "market study" was still anathema in the U.S.S.R.; today it no longer is.

A single example will suffice as an illustration. On December 16, 1958, Mr. Khrushchev reported on the Soviet agricultural situation in the following terms: "We shall no longer buy a hundredweight of wheat at from 119 to 172 rubles in the Caucasus, the Ukraine, or in Russia itself if we can obtain it for 32 rubles in Kazakhstan." The difference between 32 and 119 rubles is just too great to be dismissed on ideological grounds. As a result, the Soviet government is compelled to modify its original planning methods for the production of grain, and farmers no longer have to make compulsory deliveries. Thus the liberalization of the grain supply is not something we can impute either to ideology or Party theoreticians, but stems directly from an economic necessity. Therefore, the authorities dislike taking the responsibility for purchasing the diversified production of intensive agriculture and leave both the risk and freedom of decision making to the local authorities. Fruits and vegetables do not keep as long or cannot be transported over as long distances as grain can. This example again goes to show that liberalization is not inspired by ideological but by economic considerations.

The picture of planning as outlined by Professor Polanyi is applicable to the system of centralized economy during the Stalinist period much more than to the present-day Soviet economy, especially since the decentralization. All of Professor Polanyi's criticisms were secretly evaluated by Soviet economists; the decentralization reform of 1957 is the result of the fears and unsatisfactory results obtained till that time. The place of the market in the present Soviet economy is constantly increasing, as Professor Polanyi rightly pointed out. How can they explain that they are moving toward communism, or a purer form of communism, while at the same time a market economy is being instituted? This is a fairly simple matter. If a pair of shoes is given to everyone, and you have none, no decision is necessary; you have to take what they give you. But if two or three pairs are available, then the consumer does have a choice; in which case his tastes, whims, and probable decision all have to be taken into account. Although the consumer can be influenced to some degree, there comes a point at which one has to call upon market research, studies of the laws of elasticity, of demand, etc. The result could be a further liberalization of the Soviet economic and political systems, since the consumer will have a greater say in making his own decisions and eventually may even be able to make his opinions felt concerning factory construction, the policy of investments, etc. The evolution of Yugoslavia from a planned to a decentralized, competitive economy reinforces my optimism in this respect. As a matter of fact, it seems to me that the Soviet economy is passing through the same stages we did in Yugoslavia when we reformed our system of planning in 1950. I also think that it is evolving more slowly, doubtless because of its greater size. The logic of economic growth modifies ideological preoccupations.

I should like to add that in the area of investments there is an extremely interesting phenomenon called the "pagoda effect"; it consists of investing for the sake of investing, in order to impress various people. The expression was borrowed from the underdeveloped countries, but today pagodas are sprouting in numerous "developed" countries. The socialist countries have also practiced this kind of "conspicuous production."

I come now to the question of profits. I had the opportunity of talking with one of the men in charge of Soviet planning, who said: "The Soviet Union doesn't worry about the profits of individual enterprises, but only about the social profitability of the economy." When I asked him: "How do you calculate the social profitability of your economy?" he scratched his head and said: "Till now we haven't managed to perfect a very satisfactory system of calculating social profitability. Our efforts are currently tending in that direction."

It is true that the Soviet Union is trying to institute quantitative economic analyses which a few years back would have been regarded as a diabolical invention of capitalism. Soviet economists who belittled and scoffed at the work being done at Harvard are now trying to set up input-output charts for the Soviet Union.

To those who maintain that Soviet planning is Marxist planning, I reply by citing the authority of Strumiline, who believes that the Marxist pattern of reproduction is not at all applied to Soviet economic planning. A pragmatic plan is drawn up, it is larded with quotations from Marx, and baptized "Marxist." This is why Professor Bobrowski of Poland, an expert in the field of planning, believes Soviet planning to be made up of empirical macro-decisions. In Russia today there are differences of opinion among the planners, who constitute the Holy Order of continuity; the politicians, who are the cardinals of expediency; and the plant managers, who are the bishops of efficiency. Here then are three categories of people with varying interests, pursuing different objectives, who sometimes clash violently, while the consumers are not at all organized and the direct producers have relatively little to say about the management of their own economic activity. This situation, in which various groups of people are involved in planning, may help explain the several political tensions which plague the Soviet Union and the many differences of opinion which are evolving there.

POSTAN: I should like to begin by reiterating that, although none of us disputes the definition and analysis offered by Professor Polanyi, they seem to apply much more to the earlier than to the present stage of Soviet economy, and will apply even less in the future.

If the Soviet economy has been able to operate and continue to draw up plans—dependent on this artificial system of values—it is above all because approximately 65 per cent of production has been devoted to nonconsumer products, that is, products for which production can ignore the factor of consumer satisfaction or well-being—armaments, heavy machinery, or those intermediary products whose value is calculated not in terms of the consumer but of the producer.

Even here, of course, the fact that the finished products are not the most modern, although the classification of the intermediary products or investments is not of a sort to satisfy the factories' needs; even here the real level of this output is not the same as that which appears in the Soviet statistical planning reports. Yet this difference is not terribly obvious. In other words, production failures are not readily apparent and, in this respect, these failures constitute a peculiarity that a society can sustain so long as it expends the major portion of its effort building planes, bombs, factories, highways, and railroads. The implication here is that they characterize to a large extent a society —the Soviet society—which has evolved to a point where consumer goods are delivered to a market in which demand exceeds supply. This will always be the case as long as consumer goods remain scarce.

But if, as we are led to believe, the Soviet economy is currently evolving toward a higher proportion of production in consumer goods, it means it is giving up the situation which allows such planning to be tolerated not only by the masses but also by the leaders. If we can picture the time when the Soviet economy will catch up with and pass the American economy— and I view the future development of Western economy with sufficient pessimism so that I *can* foresee such a time—the need for this planning will disappear and the network of social relations it entails will vanish with it.

Remember that in a society which devotes the major part of production to fulfilling consumer needs and where consumer goods are so plentiful the consumer is free to choose among them, production has to rely on certain market indicators. The objective of consumer production is consumer satisfaction: this is a way of obtaining political, psychological, or emotional support from the masses, of justifying the ideological argument which in the Soviet world consists of satisfying the needs of the ordinary man.

If the Russians do manage to bring about this affluence, they will have to consider the demands—and consequently the changes and spontaneous variations—of popular taste as the basic index for determining the production structure for consumer goods. Moreover, if the output of goods is set at a high level, by the volume and structure of the production of consumer goods, even heavy industry will eventually reflect the spontaneous variations of the demands and tastes of the consumers, just as they do in capitalist societies. What is more, if the Russians wish to avoid depending entirely on these capricious variations of demand, if they reach the point of pushing production in certain areas, I am convinced they will adopt the whole advertising paraphernalia, not only market research but everything necessary to create a demand—even an artificial one —for all the pots and pans their factories will turn out. Paraphernalia, we are told, typical of the affluent Western society.

We might therefore be able to utilize the purely economic differences that W. W. Rostow envisages. In general, he differentiates the economic stages according to the nature of production. I believe that the differences are not so great, and that on certain points there are striking resemblances. I also think that the social aspects of production, or at least what we call the social aspects, are also fairly close. Professor Salin made a most judicious remark when he said that it is absurd to compare an industrial revolution in England with an industrial revolution in Timbuktu, or with one in Russia. In the Western world, the industrial revolution led to the rise of the middle classes, in Russia to the emergence of an entirely different social group, and in Timbuktu it might well give rise to still another social group.

This distinction is certainly borne out by the study of the early stages of industrial revolutions in various countries. It is more and more difficult to verify when we compare more developed economic systems. We are not like those voluntary deaf-mute Soviet delegates with whom I discussed these problems at Amsterdam; thus we know very well that, in the realms of management structure and attitude, there are not any tremendous differences between Russian and Western industry. We also know that the divorce between ownership and management, the growth of a class of skilled technicians and managers, the emergence and evolution of an industrial bureaucracy in Western Europe gave birth there to a social type which, in its recruitment methods, its attitudes and functions, is not basically different from the type of person in charge of important sectors of the Soviet economy: they are functionaries of industry and the economy. We also know that in England this particular class considers with complete equanimity the possibility that industry will be nationalized. For them, all it means is a change of title.

In this area, then, I believe that the status, importance, and attitude of this class in a country such as Soviet Russia will necessarily resemble those of comparable classes in the Western world—in Europe or in America. This resemblance can only become more pronounced as the evolution progresses; for the predominance of consumer taste—everything characteristic of an affluent society in the area of consumer goods—must of necessity give more freedom to production units than they now enjoy, as far as brands, prices, and production are concerned. This will constitute a considerable emancipation, the effects of which will be felt in the higher echelons of planning. We already see this beginning in those sectors of Soviet industry where there is an overproduction.

Can we predict that over a period of time the economy and social structure of industry—not the structure of the state or of political life, but of industry alone—will move closer together in the two blocs, to the point of absolute identity? I cannot say.

We can foresee, as W. W. Rostow has already shown, the stage which will follow that of abundance, characterized by a wave of consumer merchandise. Perhaps in the West we are already experiencing a foretaste of this next stage by the development of the taste for private life and for things not made in factories. In England, for instance, a desire for children. People prefer going without a second car, a swimming pool, or a television set to enjoy the advantages (doubtful from a purely economic viewpoint) of a third or fourth child. In France, of course, this particular form of preference is obscured by the fact that the state offers generous subsidies for large families. In England, where such preferences are penalized heavily, this change in attitude by the upper and middle classes is quite remarkable. Much of what Kennan hoped might happen is now taking place, because the higher demand groups—the middle and upper classes

—are now more than satisfied, are saturated by the abundance of consumer goods. This can therefore take place throughout the Western world.

How about in the Soviet Union? If the social element remains the same and does not follow the change in production, while the psychology changes with the saturation of the population, what will happen? To answer, or even discuss, the question, I think we have to take into account certain factors which normally do not figure in economic discussions.

I believe that the *Homo Sovieticus*—the typical man whom, according to Mr. Kennan, the Russians have succeeded in creating—is a kind of materialist, whose sense of good and evil is quite materialistic and whose standards of progress, success, and prestige seem to many to belong to the ideas of the nineteenth century.

This salient feature—the love of size—in fact, all these traits we wrongly ascribe to certain stages of the American industrial evolution may still be meaningful when the ideologies are on the point of taking over the edifice of production. Everything depends on how much will have been accomplished, and how much still remains to be done. It may be, as W. W. Rostow believes, that in Russia overdemand will be channeled toward lunar probes and huge space vehicles, but we have no idea what the outcome of this may be.

I cannot guess how great our differences will be, or how high we will ascend. Everything I say is vitiated by the fact that, according to my basic theory, a unilateral modification is enough to make two economies or societies move closer together or farther apart. Therefore, all the Russians have to do is follow a course different from ours. Yet I believe the Soviet system has developed within itself a rapid and continuing capacity for material development. However, our system of values, our political system, do not permit us to distribute one "national" product which satisfies solely the demands of the leaders, but require that the pressures of individual taste be reflected. Thus we will be unable to maintain the rate of investment at a level which would enable us to feed and support a continuous process of economic development.

There will be societies rich in material goods, others famed for their social consciousness; there will be ruined societies, and well-to-do societies devoid of any social conscience. I therefore believe that our sense of getting along together must consist of making a virtue out of necessity.

LINDBLOM: As you see, it is possible to state that central planning in the Soviet Union can, on the one hand, be a failure and, on the other, allow a very high level of production to be attained. It is a failure in the sense that it is marked by the laissez faire we are all aware of, and yet this method attains— for other reasons we can imagine—an extremely high rate of growth and a high degree of effectiveness in the military field. Thus I would wager, with some hesitation, that we may witness an even tighter control of the Soviet economy or any segment of central planning.

I believe you are right in suggesting that the principal mechanisms of the Soviet economy which we still do not understand are of a decentralized sort, similar to those you describe, which on certain points are related to the market, but are not, strictly speaking, market mechanisms.

Here, I run into one difficulty—the way we should approach these processes. First, let me take your earlier article in which you explained the notion of polycentrism and studied the flexibility of social obligations. You considered the possibilities of a kind of co-operative, mutual, noncentralized process of adjustment in which each party, at different stages, attempts to bring about an adjustment by considering the other people as data and, by following the process through, reach a solution to the problem. What you have not done, and what I should like to see you do, is consider the possibilities not as they apply to industry, where relatively technical decisions are made, but to the area of politics. I have the feeling that this kind of co-operative but profoundly decentralized process of mutual adjustment at a fairly high level of politics can explain in part the Soviet economic success and provide a more general and meaningful interpretation of this success than will the analysis of the specific mechanisms set forth in the last part of your report.

I would also like to briefly mention some other points which I was led to by my own work. If you are dealing with people who are partisan (not in the sense that they hate each other or that their interests conflict, but people who are simply indifferent to one another, who don't want to co-operate), what are the chances for their reaching a series of rational decisions in the highest echelons of government without resorting to some central control or market mechanisms to integrate them? It now becomes immediately apparent—although it took me several years to reach these conclusions—that there do exist processes which I might term "atomistic adjustments" similar to those you have described. I use the term "atomistic" for the following reason: these mechanisms are similar to the market mechanisms we refer to when we say "atomistic competition"; this is a method whereby every participant who has to make a decision at a given time considers, on his level, the others' decisions and, as a result, makes up his mind without respect for the others. The latter, whose plans are then disturbed, in turn make a decision by considering each of the others as a datum. This process, carried on indefinitely (under circumstances I do not fully fathom but which Mr. Polanyi is trying to clarify), will result in a highly rational settlement of their conflicting interests.

The second possibility is that whereby each participant refers something to the others, that is, he says to himself: "I'll only make this or that decision, which won't bother anyone." His sphere of action is therefore what we might call the chinks and crannies left by the others, those areas of freedom he can glean. This is the opposite situation from that described first.

We have a third, sort of residual, possibility in which you are no different from your fellow men, nor do you ignore them. You guess what the plausible reaction will be, anticipate it, try to control it, and act accordingly, knowing that your decision will arouse such and such a reaction. I believe this is the kind of adjustment operative in the Soviet Union on a fairly high political plane, just as it does in the Western world.

By that I do not mean to imply that other forms do not exist, among which "bargaining"—that is, the exchange of threats or promises to help or harm someone—is the only one to have been studied in the literature of recent years. I will say that bargaining, although it is the most deep-rooted, the most easily assimilated, and the most familiar of these dismembered, nonsynoptic methods of making decisions, is only one among many which your study has contributed greatly to clarify.

POLANYI: With reference to Professor Postan's remarks, may I say that, in regard to public ownership (this of course is pure speculation) one thing we must realize is that while legal ownership of the enterprise adds nothing to the scope of the control, it reduces the possibilities of operations and excludes the market of capital. Thus when we speculate about the utopian situation of the future when we will have universal ownership of industry by the state, there will be no more capital market. Will there be other differences? First, I believe that we would be wrong to speak lightly of the state of abundance, because one can always distribute a real demand which will reduce the abundance to a scarcity of goods as compared with the prevailing demand. This question is discussed quite apart from the problem Kornai raises. He asks would it really not be possible to operate on the profit principle? Instead of operating as we do on the basis of a global product, could we not consider net production instead of the gross production we now base our figures on? We can only move in this direction, Kornai says, if we have a system of prices which are autonomous and can be adjusted by bargaining. In this case, of course, I find it difficult to see what are the grounds for the dynamism and enthusiasm which Mr. Khrushchev sincerely inspires when he rejects—as he is currently doing—the influences and temptations of an American *ambiance*. I cannot imagine how this system can survive by voluntarily allowing prices to be manipulated by the enterprises; this would preclude any meaningful control by the government, except in the area of investments, which under these circumstances would be of relatively little importance.

I don't know the answer to this problem; I merely wanted to expose some of its facets to your attention, leaving each of you to formulate his own hypotheses.

ARON: The discussion seems to have taken place on several different planes. There was an entirely abstract plane—an evaluation of the values as they exist in the West and in the Soviet world, and Polanyi's basic premise that this comparison of values gave rise to errors and misunderstandings, because in one case the frame of reference was the preference and choice of the individual, whereas in the other there was simply a global quantitative evaluation of the physical goods produced, suppression of the freedom of choice, and of the variety of merchandise. This, Polanyi suggests, represents a reduction as compared to the values one would find in a Western estimate. But as I listened to Michael Polanyi I kept wondering what a Soviet economist would say to him in reply. With his permission, I shall answer for a Soviet economist I know who explained to me why the choice should not be left to the consumer and why an economy produced more values when consumers were not free to choose. I must say that his reply is a Platonic one, that is, that those who govern know what is good for the governed. Those who govern know in what order various merchandise should be manufactured; they know just what people should be given at each stage of their economic development. If they are given a certain type of merchandise too early, the fact that a minority has the capacity to choose not only does not represent an increase in the over-all value, but a decrease. For the decision as to which type of merchandise to produce is an aspect of the educational effort in the Soviet Union between the rulers and the people. And this leads me to the next thought: there is a point at which a purely economic analysis of value ceases and the philosophical problem of what should properly be called "value" begins. In other words, the economic calculations which Polanyi uses are meaningless for someone who believes in a different philosophy. Personally, I doubt that the Soviets would accept the autonomy of the economic order in the Western sense of this term.

The second and more simple plane on which our discussion took place was the attempt to determine how the Soviet regime worked and what changes we might expect to see in the system. Third, we tried to evaluate the possibilities of a *rapprochement* between the systems. The fourth area of discussion, which was marked by Professor Postan's interesting and cogent observations, dealt with the time when, after all the economies had attained a certain degree of affluence, a new choice would be opened up to various societies. Diversity would re-enter the picture because of the new possibilities offered. One can, with a little imagination, take today's diversity for the choice of the stages of economic growth, then a diversity in the distance, on our historical horizon, at the time when the entire world will have attained a certain affluence, and the question will be posed: what do we do with it? At no time is the economic order autonomous in its rationality with regard to individual preferences within a society and with regard to philosophies.

CHAPTER II: THE "THIRD WORLD" AND THE INDUSTRIAL SOCIETY

KENNAN: I should like to comment on the second of Aron's questions concerning the suitability of Western and Soviet political institutions respectively to the needs of peoples of underdeveloped countries.

If I am not mistaken, I think I detect in his paper a note of keen concern over the possibility that the Western example may prove really unsuitable to these needs and that, as he puts it, a concern for man's well-being, in the countries concerned, will involve subjecting him to state tyranny and systematic falsehoods. I wonder whether it is not a bit exaggerated to think in such clear-cut terms.

Let us remember, first of all, that authoritarianism, in one form or another, has been throughout the ages the normal lot of mankind. It is true that people of my generation in America were brought up to believe that liberal democracy, on the Anglo-Saxon pattern, was the final product of political enlightenment— a system which had a potential universal validity and to which all societies ought properly to tend.

But the events of the past forty years have taught us better. Today, many of us would be inclined to regard our own institutions as at best a happy aberration, enjoyed by certain people who had their political origins on the shores of the English Channel and the North Sea, connected specifically with the traditions of mercantile sea power rather than land power, of doubtful

122

applicability in a wider geographic sphere, and plainly subject to the discipline of evolution in time. We could attach, therefore, no absolute positive value to these institutions, much as we may cherish them ourselves.

And conversely, just as we would attribute no absolute positive value to our own institutions, so we could attribute no absolute negative value to those of the Russians. These latter, as we have just noted, are now embraced in a process of evolution. They are changing, and we cannot yet know the full measure of the change. And besides, the differences that divide these institutions from our own are relative, not absolute.

Aron does well to single out the one-party regime, the suppression of criticism, and the systematic cultivation of falsehood as features of Soviet power that contrast basically with what we have in the West.

But the deliberate cultivation of falsehood seems to me to be undergoing, as a governmental policy, a process of severe erosion. The temper of Soviet youth and the pressures of the time are against it. I can't imagine that it can be long continued in the manner of the past. And as for the one-party system, it must be contrasted, unfortunately, with precisely that segment in the political life of the West which is itself today most subject to question, most doubtful in point of adequacy to the needs of the time—the system of political parties and the institutions through which they find expression. In the doctrinal sense, we in America also have in certain respects a one-party system; for the two parties are ideologically undistinguishable, their pronouncements form one integral body of banality and platitude. Whoever does not care to work within their common framework is also condemned, like the nonparty person in Russia, to political passivity, to an internal emigration.

I would not like to be misunderstood at this point. I would be the last to deny the validity of relative distinctions. I find our system, for all its shortcomings, vastly preferable to that which confronts it on the communist side, if only because it interposes no political barriers to the freedom of the mind.

But from the standpoint of the underdeveloped people, seeking inspiration and example, this relativity is significant, and spares them the necessity of hard and fast choices. It seems to me overwhelmingly likely that there are going to be in the future as many forms of government in this world as there are genuine national entities. No single pattern—as is already evident in the communist orbit—need be, or will be, universally imposed. Admittedly, the personality of the full-blown totalitarian state is an international problem, in the long run intolerable to the security of the neighboring states and to the interests of world peace. But for the endless varieties and gradations of normal authoritarianism, we in the West can afford to manifest a relaxed and sympathetic tolerance.

We may hope, for the sake of the comfort of other peoples—in order, that is, that they may not be obliged to treat each other like beasts—that they will find political institutions which preserve them from a wholly arbitrary system of justice and which establish some relationship, however imperfect, between the popular will and the means by which power is transferred from one set of hands to another. These are, after all, the most essential virtues of our own institutions.

But we need not be in a hurry; and above all, we need not see ourselves defeated, and declare ourselves in advance defeated, if the institutions of others do not immediately meet these requirements. It is in this direction, after all, that the communist countries are themselves moving. There is no reason why the peoples of Africa and Asia, even if they feel the need of a strong authoritarian power in the early phases of industrialization, should feel obliged to grope back into the horrors of Stalinism for their inspiration. Stalin, after all, was not really so successful as the industrializer of Russia. It was Khrushchev who, with a greater liberality and confidence of approach, really succeeded in unleashing the full flood of Russian economic power.

MEHTA: When we speak of the "third world" I think it would be most unfortunate if we were to consider it as an undifferentiated whole. Certain parts of it can most likely be compared to others, but there are some which, for various reasons, should be the shapers of their own destinies. In fact, I think my country inevitably ought to be the author of its own destiny. Conditions in India are such that it cannot hope to become an integral part of either the Western or communist orbit.

When we talk about democracy, we should make one point quite clear straight off: in India, for example, a number of frightful things have occurred which fill us with shame. In fact, it is probable that during the bloody and troubled period we went through in India more people were killed by the police than in most other countries. Yet the fact remains that in India there exists an abiding faith in democracy and a way of affirming and reaffirming it time and again by a method we call civil disobedience. This practice enables the people to participate in the affairs of state in ways unknown even in Switzerland. The participation takes the form not of referendums or the designation of governments at set periods, but by the direct, nonviolent action of the population itself. It thus becomes quite impossible for any government whatever to apply a given policy if large segments of the population are hostile to it.

Recently, for example, the communist government of Kerala was obliged to resign because of the massive popular opposition. No arms were used, but 2 per cent of the adult population faced the risk of going to jail.

This same thing has happened in many states. At times civil disobedience makes it difficult for an official to put a long-range policy into effect. But this resistance does exercise an actual control and makes democracy so real that I doubt such an instrument exists anywhere else. This is a product of a specific country. It has not occurred in China, Japan, or Pakistan, but it has appeared in India. This is how we won our freedom, and this is how we plan to keep it.

In the course of my trips between Egypt and Indonesia I have met many people on all social levels and I have reached the conclusion—which is hard to relinquish—that in these countries, as in India, the democratic ideal burns brightly, even if the Army has taken over the government. The democratic institutions of a given Western country are not necessarily accepted today as they once were. Almost automatically, the British colonies instinctively adopted British institutions. American colonies probably adopted American institutions. The same thing might have happened with the French colonies. Today it is no longer a question of automatic acceptance, but of trying to determine which institutions are most suited to the needs and talents of the various people. Yet allegiance to democratic ideals persists. As Professor Rostow has observed, an attempt is made to lend legitimacy to power, and this has to take root in the popular will. A form has to be given; there have to be the opportunity and the means for the sovereignty of the people to assert itself at last. This solution is accepted in Pakistan, Burma, and Egypt, whether it is practiced or not; the leaders accept it, for they are content only if they are subjected to the control and approval of the people. It is quite likely that the present leaders of Pakistan have more solid popular support than did the previous regime, which was elected. But this is not enough. In speaking with them, one feels they have the impression they are desecrating what they consider to be "the good life." It's a little like the woman who believes she has everything, except purity. This idea that the democratic ideal automatically assures political purity is a valuable fact for Asia, in numerous regions, and should be borne in mind.

The third point I should like to mention is that nationalism began as a force directed against the Western powers. But this same phenomenon has now taken cognizance of the communist danger. This is especially true about China, which is a nation-state and not a social state; it is perhaps a state in the process of development, but essentially a nation-state. This is causing considerable concern today, and there is a growing feeling in India, as well as in the neighboring countries of Nepal and Burma, and probably in Pakistan, that the challenge of China must be met. I say the challenge of China and not of communism, for insofar as China identifies herself with communism, communism suffers in India and Burma. In return, communism can survive, with difficulty, in France, or probably in Italy, in spite of the challenge offered by nationalism.

The identification of communism with a powerful state which threatens our existence creates a new element in the picture. This does not mean that we turn and embrace the West, but merely that we are trying to discover what is best for us. We can no longer accept one or the other of the world's dichotomies; for us, neither the Western nor the communist world any longer has any meaning. The former has caused us to suffer for almost two centuries; the latter is threatening the new generation. Four hundred million Indians are trying to discover the national well-springs of power. The fact that nationalism is fast becoming a force which will bow neither to communism nor the West creates a wholly new situation. Yet in this new situation the question which is posed about Egypt in Indonesia is that a legal, orderly state is not enough. President Nasser and President Ayub Khan can offer us examples of orderly, irreproachably legal states. In Pakistan today there is no discontent on this score, but both Presidents Nasser and Ayub Khan realize—as do their people—that law and order do not suffice. The state has to be built, the population awakened and aroused, that is, one has to organize and whip up enthusiasm, and this is precisely what the communists have managed to do when they develop a country. The principal contribution of the communists is that, in a short space of time, they have created efficient organizations and aroused such enthusiasm that tasks which normally take a long time have been accomplished in much shorter periods.

Is the multiparty state able to arouse enthusiasm, does it constitute a framework conducive to organization, or, on the contrary, does it not tend to distort or even destroy the qualities of organization and dampen the enthusiasm of the people? This is why—although in my own country I am a member of the opposition—I have expressed an opinion which Professor Aron later characterized as "a government without alternative." You can have all the freedom you want, but for fifteen or twenty years "a government without alternative." There are elections, of course, but a government enjoys such a majority that it cannot be overthrown, even if it is a coalition government. This is the usefulness of civil disobedience. Some people would be inclined to accept a "government without alternative" on the condition that they would be accorded complete freedom on the issues that are especially dear to them.

It would therefore be wrong for political science to envisage only two types of states, one with a single party and complete suppression of liberty and the other with several parties with a great deal of freedom. It may be that these two sorts of states are unsuitable for underdeveloped countries, and that we are on the point of discovering a form of government adapted to our needs. This form, as I have indicated, may be "a government without alternative" which by various means may grant considerable rights and freedom to its citizens.

I would like to raise a final point: in India and perhaps in Pakistan and Indonesia there is the danger that the industrial society may constitute a more or less autonomous sector. This danger may never come to pass, for in the West and perhaps in the communist world the industrial society has not penetrated into every area of economic and social life. And yet the danger exists that this society will form a separate entity, a sort of isolated fraction or superstructure, and as such play a role not unlike that of imperialism vis-à-vis the colonial countries. From a situation such as this an internal imperialism can grow, with an industrial society which would make up the superstructure and a base of agriculture in which the rural society would be neglected and grow stagnant. I note that in India, where resources are at a premium and the population is extremely high, production is not evaluated in terms of men but of land—not per capita but per acre. This distinction lends special significance to communal life, for it is not man and his instruments that matter, nor his tools and techniques, but the need for organization, the necessity to derive the maximum from resources other than human resources, which can be deployed. Our job is to find out whether more emphasis should not be placed on communal life, and this leads us straight to an important question.

Mr. Kennan's speech was a source of great encouragement to me, for if the most developed countries such as the United States were to express themselves in the same terms as his— on the question under discussion, of course—our task would be simple. If modernism—for, after all, is it not modernism which is presently casting doubts about traditional societies— were judged solely as a form of unlimited development, I think that all societies would end up being completely destroyed. Admittedly, modernism can be considered as a form of development, which in fact is necessary for a while, but a certain amount of stability is also indispensable. If traditional societies such as those we have in Asia are thought of as the thesis, and industrial society as the antithesis, there is a synthesis which is on the verge of absorbing a considerable portion of the wisdom and equilibrium of the traditional societies. Our task then becomes easy. The communist challenge is strictly the challenge of the antithesis; there is no middle term. This is why the traditional society has to be broken, destroyed. In India we have often had the feeling—perhaps as a result of a peculiar combination of national resources, a certain culture, and a certain civilization which has lasted for centuries and played a major role in our recent political struggles—that this combination is indissolubly linked to the renaissance of India. This is perhaps also true of Pakistan and Indonesia. A close connection exists between the renaissance of India in the nineteenth and in the twentieth century.

This renaissance was in part characterized by modernism and also by an effort to awaken, and stir up renewed interest in, some of the great achievements of the past. This would seem to indicate that development is a necessary but insufficient dimension. This is an extremely difficult notion to make hungry people understand, people whose most elementary needs remain unfulfilled. There is another dimension which is useful to us—culture, a certain harmony, a certain comprehension. This harmony and comprehension will help us enormously to create a new society which will facilitate the assimilation of numerous aspects of the industrial society; otherwise we will not succeed in ridding our people of poverty and filth. It does not follow that we shall have to solve problems identical to those that some of you have to solve today. Once poverty and filth have been eliminated, the warning and vision which Professor Kennan presented will take shape and become an integral part of what we call modernism. Then we shall be able to transcend the conflict between the West and the communist world, and in this connection I think we will help eliminate the difficulties that at least a third of the world has to face today. I therefore believe that our task would be greatly advanced if, during this seminar or other similar meetings of Western intellectuals, more attention were paid to the very important point elucidated by Professor Kennan.

I want it understood, however, that I am not making any reproaches. Our country has borrowed heavily from the West. If we condemned British domination, it was because it seemed contrary to the British spirit. Certain democratic ideas and certain Western institutions have deep roots in my country, because for eighty years we were directly involved with them. We have also more or less modeled our constitution and political institutions on those of the West. Our judicial power remains independent and the press is largely free. This is a very important point. Finally, we are vitally interested in the application of science to economic problems.

Now a few comments about Mr. Aron's paper. As for the future of the underdeveloped countries and the paths open to them, he writes that the desire for independence means the delusive desire for a better life. This is an untenable thesis. You speak of the Asiatic method of production. I concede that there is a grave danger there, a sort of excrescence impregnated with modernism. For me, this represents internal imperialism.

I do not believe that a billion, or even slightly more than a billion, people—that is, from 40 to 50 per cent of the world's population—can live in such a state that nine-tenths of the society are poverty stricken and one-tenth lives decently. This, as I have already stated, is an impossible situation. If one excludes both solutions—communist and liberal—the only one left is the third. But even that choice is difficult, not for ideological but for purely materialistic reasons. In our part of the world, there is no place for communism. I do not have time to go into detail, but it is astonishing how little attention was paid to the events in Kerala and to the Kerala government. This government failed in its efforts to solve the fundamental problems of the country. What is more, in its efforts to impose a type of society it provoked an explosion which toppled the regime. You may say that this was only a limited experiment in communization, but I maintain that it should help us understand certain basic difficulties. Take India: there are 300,000,000 peasants, of whom 50 to 70 per cent own less than an acre of land. Annual income is fifty-six dollars. These are the cold, cruel facts; they make any application of a communist solution difficult. You'll understand that a third solution has to be found.

Now the question of our population: whether we talk of India, Pakistan, or Indonesia, we are dealing with a land, a society, and people who have suffered the effects of erosion. Where then do we begin? In my opinion, the only way to solve the problem is not to remake our soil or our society, but to remake our people. The whole process has to be reversed. We cannot hope to remake our economy if we don't improve our people. Only better men will be able to confront this terrible challenge that neither the West—where the population and resources developed together—nor the Soviet Union—so rich in natural resources—nor the United States had to contend with. In our part of the world resources are limited, and there is a vast population which for many reasons is not easy to control. Thus we have to approach the problem from a different angle. Through technology? I don't know. Others will decide; we have experts in every area, but my feeling is that technology has generally progressed, while in the countries of Asia it will be conditioned by sociology. It will not dictate social conditions, but will have to submit to the needs of our society. The same with science. In other words, we have to organize and slow down the development of technology or our society will be completely destroyed. Communism allows this, claiming that in thirty or forty years we can arrive at a new stability. If we let ourselves be seduced by this evolution, it would perhaps be the greatest tragedy that any group of people has ever known. Thus the discovery of technological "locks" would help us regulate the influx of techniques in terms of our needs and for us this is of major importance.

Our population is largely rural, and in all probability we will tend to evolve in the direction of rural industrial communities. But the minute we think of rural industrial communities, we also have to think of local markets. A great number of these markets have to be grouped into a larger market. This is a very different conception from either a communist or a capitalist economy. These things call for long and careful reflection.

Take politics. We speak of politics when there are parties, and perhaps there is no difference between them and the parties have to make an effort to ferret some out. The people may be apathetic because there are really no issues. But, on the other hand, there is the one-party system. We find ourselves in a very different situation. If we cannot accept the monolithic party, which would not serve our purposes, it would be equally dangerous to offer ourselves the luxury of a multiparty regime which would try to discover nonexistent differences. Thus we have to come up with a policy based on a conscious unanimity; a policy through which, when we draw up our plans every five years, for example, we try to arrive at unanimity. This calls for much greater vigilance on our part than mere opposition or exercise of choice. A determined effort for over-all comprehension is required. It is not so much the institutions that matter as man, his attitude and viewpoint. As I foresee the future of our section of the world, we will raise our living standards, but they will still remain low compared to those of the West and the communist countries. But we shall have to remedy this weakness—a low economic level—if we want to avoid the exodus of the very people we have to rely on to rebuild our society. Caught between the two giants of the communist and Western blocs, we must, I believe, adopt a middle course, and this is precisely what Mr. Kennan has suggested for the European countries, if I understood him correctly. Caught between the two atomic, hydrogen-bomb powers—the United States and the Soviet Union—the European countries must reject military technique and adapt themselves to a new technique, as Mr. Kennan proposed in his now famous lectures. But this new technique, presented in his lecture on the military future, would require a change in military preparations.

Mr. Aron has also spoken of a change. But for him this mutation is the last link of the chain; for us it is merely a means. What, in his view, is the final link? It is the basis on which to build the very foundations of our march forward, without which we shall be swallowed up. This basic, or as you call it "historic," mutation is not an ideology, not something for proselytizing; it is functional; without it we cannot survive, we cannot progress, we are helpless. It is a condition of progress, not the ultimate goal. Mr. Kennan has emphasized this point by stating that we have reached the stage when men of good will must act. This is why communism is helpless in India. How can it reach half a million villages? A major party cannot be created in a day. In China a great party was forged by the revolution. Other major parties can be or are born of revolutions in other countries. But it is simply impossible, through normal channels, to forge a great party, to reach and galvanize millions of men in half a million villages. This galvanization must begin on the spiritual level. This is where the men of good will come in. When we listen to Mr. Kennan, we have the impression that Russia is going to evolve in a certain direction. I am considerably heartened by this new shift in thinking, because I think it will have an effect on the Russians themselves. If we keep on saying that the Russians can only behave badly, we will encourage them to behave badly. There is such a thing as the emanation of the heart, and it is not an ideological concept. For Mr. Kennan, this is perhaps the culmination of America's rise to prominence; for us, it is a rock on which we will be able to build the church of our future. As Marx deemed that he had to set Hegel's thinking aright, I too often have the impression that a great number of things said here have to be modified or interpreted if they are to have any meaning for the people of my country.

I feel that the world dialogue would be much more meaningful if we clearly understood that, although our image of man and society, and our conception of the ideal society inhabited by men of good will scarcely differs, the paths leading to it, the ascents and descents, curves and plateaus, are so different that unless we learn how to reconcile them, this world's topography will lose a great deal of its interest and meaning.

ARON: Mr. Asoka Mehta has in a sense accused me of undue pessimism in my view of the underdeveloped countries. He is right, because my report, although seemingly objective, is closely linked to my personality, prejudices, and passions. When I discussed the underdeveloped countries, I talked about them—as he has said—with a sort of despair, in that I saw the perfectly inadmissable aspect of all the possibilities that seem to lie before us. It is impossible for two-thirds of mankind to continue living in growing poverty while one-third has extricated itself from it. It is unthinkable for colonial domination to continue on the premise that to eliminate it would deprive the region of the modernized sector of industry. But it is also a fact that in certain countries I know fairly well, such as North Africa, the end of colonial domination did coincide with the departure of the most modern elements of industry, raising the specter that political liberation might bring with it a further aggravation of the economic situation. On the other hand, in Asian countries the historical change necessary to institute modern production methods requires such far-reaching social and psychological transformations that one hesitates over the decisive question as to what type of government will make this historical change possible. And yet I am thoroughly convinced, as is Mr. Kennan and all the rest of us, that the choice between Stalinist totalitarianism and parliamentary democracy is absurd; there are many possible intermediary forms. But Mr. Asoka Mehta's words quite convinced me that the people of India are deeply concerned not so much with intermediate political forms as with the human and spiritual change which will render the introduction of the elements indispensable to the industrial society possible in India without its leading to despotism in government and even without its leading, as Mr. Mehta stated, to the industrial society. It is both inevitable and indispensable that industry and certain paraphernalia of industrial production be instituted, but this does not necessarily mean that Indian society will coincide with or resemble either the Russian or American industrial societies. The distinction between industry and industrial society was certainly a key point in our discussions, although it constitutes a different language from the one I used.

SALIN: I agree completely with Mr. Kennan that the place occupied today by the theory of growth is as much a matter of fashion as was the importance accorded twenty years ago to the theory of nations. And yet we cannot escape the task of maintaining economic growth, because it is an indispensable attribute of consumer-oriented capitalist societies, and because we have preached the gospel of economic growth to the underdeveloped countries. This gospel is contrary to what the Moslem countries have always believed; in spite of what our colleague from India has said, it is also contrary to the Indian way of life as it has been lived for centuries, and to Gandhi's teaching. Today the underdeveloped countries are beginning to believe this new gospel imported from Europe or America; this is why the search for growth is at once an intellectual vogue and a political and economic reality we have to take into consideration. From the eighteenth or nineteenth century on, it was no longer possible to preach that it is easier for a camel to pass through the needle's eye than for a rich man to enter the kingdom of heaven; as soon as people began to believe that on the contrary the accumulation of wealth was the path to the kingdom of heaven, there was nothing one could do, except put into effect a social policy. So today, if we want to avoid a general collapse, we ought to question ourselves seriously as to which system— Western or Soviet—is better adapted to the conditions of industrialization for the underdeveloped countries. Here again, as in his analysis of the future evolution of Russia, I'm afraid Mr. Kennan was a trifle optimistic. While in principle there is no reason why power has to imply terror in these countries, in practice this still remains to be proved. This hinges on the question of whether masses which for a millennium and a half have not been raised in the Judaic-Christian ethos of work can be made to work regularly and systematically, and whether it is possible both to preserve Indian communal life and enter into the world of industry and mass society.

ARON: The problem we were basically concerned with is that today there is a certain scientific or rational method of work organization which is subjected to the law of productivity. Among the social consequences it implies are urbanization, industrialization, and a different division of labor compared with that common to agricultural societies of the past. In Europe, this scientifically organized method of production has been the result of a complex historical process which included changes in the way of thinking, feeling, and in the organization of society. The secularization of thought and a certain attitude toward this world were responsible for the historical process which led to what I called industrial society. Several participants have noted, and everyone agrees, that in the West this method of work organization was bound up with a complex of beliefs and social structures. Messrs. Del Corral and Salin stressed this point. But once this rational system of production is set up, it seems to be, and actually is, transferable. Certain of its features are without a doubt transferable, and it seems likely that it can be transferred to non-Westerners. Whether or not we should use the word "inevitable" or "indispensable" seems to me of secondary importance, because I think that from the nineteenth century on this method of organizing production came to be the condition for power.

It is striking that the non-Western country which most successfully borrowed this system, that is, Japan, did so basically for reasons of security and national power. The Japanese were the first to realize that the only way to maintain their independence and national sovereignty was to borrow the West's methods of work organization. Today, another factor besides power has entered the picture: this organizational method seems to be the condition *sine qua non* in the struggle against poverty. Now, when a certain method of social organization appears as the condition both for power and wealth, it seems absolutely inconceivable to me that other societies will fail to want it. For although some individuals may disdain this world or remain indifferent to wealth or power, societies and civilizations in general have never chosen ineffectiveness or poverty. The problem is knowing what in this Western system is necessary for power and wealth. To the extent that this economic system is the condition for power, it assumes a value, or is thought of as having a value, precisely because it is what men want.

As to what has to be borrowed for power and wealth, there is a doubt and a certainty. Again, consider the case of Japan. Japan is the only country which has consciously tried to ponder the problem we are considering here: what are the elements that have to be taken over from the West for us to obtain what the West has, and we want—power and wealth. With extraordinary ingenuity, the Japanese concluded that they would have to borrow the system of universal education, a certain legal system, and a certain way of organizing relations between people. In other words, the revolution of the Meiji era began with the premise that in order to resist the West the economy would have to be Westernized, and concluded that the legal and political systems also had to be Westernized. The Japanese realized that within the framework of Western society variations did exist, that is, each country adopted somewhat varying forms to assume the charges and obligations common to Western society as a whole. The result is a fascinating experiment for the sociologist: in a country such as Japan we find certain elements taken from Germany—certain technical processes for example, but not all, for Japanese mining methods are borrowed from the French. In the Japanese legal system we can find elements of the French, the German, and sometimes the English juridical systems. Recognizing that there were various modalities, the Japanese tried in each case to take what seemed best suited to their needs.

The case of Japan goes even further, for in Japan today we can observe two kinds of borrowings. There are those with historical precedents, where certain institutions and customs are taken over because they are connected with a country with the highest prestige. Thus they have adopted some customs that to us seem deplorable, for the simple reason that because they are imported from the United States they assume a special value. The extreme, pathological case of this is the striptease, which is all the rage in Japan because it comes from the United States. In this instance, a custom is adopted because it enjoys a certain prestige since it derives from a highly esteemed society.

The other case is to borrow the basic elements of economic organization. Between these two extremes—the adoption of the scientific apparatus on the one hand and the striptease on the other—lies the political problem. What political institutions ought to be taken over from the West is the question we have been debating, and this is a twofold problem: there is the problem of knowing what to adopt and also what the dynamics of economic Westernization will lead to. What to adopt is basically a question of historical timing. Parliamentary democracy as practiced in England or America was much more highly considered fifty years ago than it is today. At that time people wanted to adopt these political institutions because they seemed good. Today, people are less sure they want them; they have lost some of their luster, either because the Soviet Union has made other institutions fashionable or because there is some doubt as to whether these institutions are best suited to the established goal of new societies—the struggle against ineffectiveness and poverty.

CHAPTER III: POLITICS AND ECONOMICS

JOUVENEL: I take the floor by invoking the empirical law of conferences: the less satisfactory the introductory paper the more lively the ensuing discussion. And our discussion has to be good, because the subject is of major importance. Raymond Aron has defined it very aptly as the contradiction between attitudes applicable to technical problems and those applicable to the realm of politics. I might define it as the conflict between the principle of efficacity, which is limited but precise, and the principle of legitimacy, which is richer but more vague. I shall begin by what Böhm-Bawerk has called a "productive detour."

One word has found its way into every language: "productivity." It denotes a relation between a tangible, provable result obtained and the means—likewise tangible and provable—used to obtain it. The word is also commonly used to designate the concern about and art of increasing this ratio. Since the same causes produce the same results, it becomes immediately apparent that this ratio can only increase if all the causes contributing to the result are not entered in the denominator; scholars would say that the causes inscribed in the denominator are material causes, and these can produce a greater result through the action of an efficient cause (or a group of efficient causes), the effect of which is in fact measured by the increase of the ratio.

The efficient cause can be called the "way of operating," a

broad general notion which embraces a more restricted and precise notion of "technique." The technique is that part of the operating procedure which can be described graphically and imitated exactly. One technique is said to be superior to another when, under given circumstances, it produces better results with the same means (or an equivalent set of means) or produces the same results with fewer means.

It is obvious that the principle we are defining here is an old intellectual acquaintance, Maupertius' principle, which states that "Nature always takes the simplest routes" (we would say "the most economic"). With Maupertius this was an explicative principle (applied to Nature), but today it is directive (applied to combined human actions).

For several generations, man's psychological and intellectual evolution has been characterized by a growing penchant for action, a feeling that man is made manifest and fulfills himself by "doing" rather than by "being." He also displays a marked preference for what can be measured. It is therefore natural that his dominant concern should be with those methods of operation likely to produce the best possible results under given conditions. And we may say that the motto of the modern world is to change techniques as soon as a more efficient one has been discovered.

The newness of this frame of mind should be underscored. Throughout history, all productive activities were considered "arts" which a good artist or artisan (the two terms were long interchangeable) practiced and had to practice "according to the rules of the art," so much so that anyone who failed to follow the rules was regarded as dishonoring his trade. "Respectability" consisted of remaining faithful to traditional techniques; today, such practice is adjudged guilty of falling into a rut. Anyone who used to alter the set method was "spoiling the trade"; today, anyone who doesn't change is "an obstacle in the way of progress." The comparison is too obvious to require further explanation. Suffice it to say that a certain moral halo used to be attached to established practice, whereas today the value of a method or technique is measured solely in terms of its results.

Given the social importance of economic activities, it is inevitable that, if the slogan of efficiency prevails in that area, it will spread throughout the social mentality and affect its judgments.

Never have the public authorities so affected the lives of individuals or the evolution of society as they do today. In countries whose institutions have been long established—I am thinking of the Western democracies—the procedures used by administrative bodies to put decisions into effect are burdened by routine. Hence the common remark that public institutions and administrative methods have to be modernized.

As man's preoccupation and fascination with the concept of efficiency has grown, so has his concern with this problem. Quite recently a high French magistrate launched an attack against the judiciary routine itself.

And yet there is good reason why there is a good deal of routine in public procedures, or more exactly why they seem to be relatively stable by comparison with the rapid transformation of techniques in other areas.

Efficiency is no ideal slogan in the game of political institutions. Here the term "expeditious justice" is revealing. One may say that a system of expeditious justice is highly "productive" because the courts settle a great number of cases at a time. And yet we do not doubt that a regular system is preferable. If, however, the sole task of the judiciary were to liquidate the enemies of those in power, we would not consider the problem in the same light. By extension, if one believes that the aim of legislation is to eliminate the obstacles in the way of the people's progress along clearly defined lines, then legislation itself should be forged in an expeditious manner, and all procedural methods granted the opposition will be a waste of time with respect to this progress.

As soon as there is no doubt (or that one thinks there is no doubt) about the results desired, the means required to measure them, and the price they entail, then the maxim of efficient technique must naturally reign. We then find ourselves faced with a problem of minimizing the cost or producing the maximum results. This sort of problem doubtless can arise with public officials, but as long as the problem is so stated it is "technical" rather than "political."

To offer a simple example of the contrast between a "technical problem" and a "political problem," imagine a group of tourists, all of whom have to travel in one vehicle. Together they study their entire itinerary for the following day. First let us assume that they are all agreed as to the places they want to visit in the course of the day; they then try to work out together the most economic route linking all these points. The problem is technical. Moreover, since the problem is obviously a technical one, and there is no ambiguity about it, the people involved will no doubt find it both reasonable and economic to let one or several of their qualified members work it out among themselves; in short, turn the problem over to technicians or experts.

Now let us take this same group and assume that this time they have to cover a maximum distance during the day, that one part of the group wants to visit such and such a ruin, another a certain dam, and that it is impossible to include both places in the itinerary. The problem now becomes political, because of the varying judgments of the interested parties and their differences of opinion.

Because the term "political problem" includes the word "problem," it suggests the idea of a "solution." In school we were always given problems that had solutions. They were usually presented in the following form: the terms listed certain conditions to be met, the solution had to satisfy all these conditions, and we were assured that there was at least one solution. The terms of a political problem, on the contrary, include conditions all of which cannot be satisfied, such as the visit to the dam and the ruin. Such a problem cannot be solved; it can only be settled.

This settlement usually takes place by the application of principles according to a certain procedure. It would be pleasant to think that principles suffice, but a single historical example will show that such is not the case. After World War I, the frontier of Upper Silesia had to be drawn between a reconstituted Poland and Germany. The principle by which a people has the right to dispose of its own destiny was invoked, and accordingly a plebiscite was held, with conflicting results in different localities. By ruling out local minorities (an important oversight that we will not go into here), a map could be marked with black dots for those towns where the Germans had a majority and white dots for the towns with a Polish majority. Then it simply became a matter of drawing a line with all the black dots to the west, in German territory, and all the white dots to the east, in Polish territory. Unfortunately, it proved impossible to draw such a line. In spite of a principle, the right of people to dispose of their own fate, and of an agreement not to count local minorities, there was still no solution. Thus the line had to be drawn arbitrarily.

A political problem does not therefore admit of a set solution; its settlement is, in the final analysis, arbitrary. Whence the supreme importance of the procedures for settlement. We should give careful thought to what it is we ask of political procedures. Given that the interested parties have irreconcilable views, the arrangement cannot possibly satisfy both parties, and perhaps will not fully satisfy either. It therefore behooves us to make sure the settlement is respectable as to its method of adoption. If the procedures inspire respect, the chances will be greatly enhanced that the injured party will find the arrangement satisfactory. It is not, however, an easy matter for procedures to inspire respect: this is dependent less upon its excellence as judged by an impartial observer than upon custom. This explains the "routine" feature of governmental procedures we have already compared with the successive transformation of methods characteristic of a technical society.

It is certain that the frequent change of procedures destroys their prestige. An American can speak with respect, even with love, of his constitution; a Frenchman cannot. There is not the slightest doubt but that the successive changes in balloting methods in France since the end of World War I have helped discredit the representative system, as the disdain of parliamentary forms by the French deputies themselves has caused both the forms and the members of parliament to be the subject of derision. Needless to say, this is a most regrettable state of affairs.

It is therefore necessary that political forms appear not to change even when they do. It is quite true that British elections have for all practical purposes become a plebiscite in favor of the parliamentary team, leader of a victorious party, so that Parliament is no longer sovereign except in name. It is also true that under President Eisenhower the executive power, which the Constitution delegates to a single chief, assumed the character of a polysynod. And yet, in both cases the illusion persists that the political systems remain unchanged.

I cannot take up here the reasons which cause a political system to evolve. Let me simply point out two facts: the first is the considerable difference between the theory of a system and its practice; the second is that the system is never given a general overhaul in order to improve its efficiency. It evolves in a quasi-occult way, or it jumps, but it is never periodically and systematically overhauled as is a system where efficiency is law.

From these two preceding statements there follow important consequences for what we call "New States"—a strange epithet, for some of them already existed when there were nothing but tribes in Europe. The essential difference between these people and those of the West is their lag in technique. These societies are still linked to hallowed economic methods, which their leaders want to modernize by instilling the modern spirit, namely, the concern for more efficient methods.

These people are also undergoing a change in the political

sphere, and this change has in fact been much more sudden than the technical mutation can ever be. A political change has taken place by the advent of political teams who have won or restored their country's sovereignty. By so doing they have displayed proof of political efficiency. It goes without saying that this political efficiency does not necessarily imply administrative efficiency; the two may or may not be allied. It also goes without saying that the methods used to win independence are not generally suitable for setting up national governmental procedures.

Thus "New States" are faced with a major problem of organizing governmental and administrative procedures. We Westerners offer these countries our models and say to them: "Take our methods, but also take our procedures." But the political-administrative systems of the major Western states are historical mixtures of efficiency and legitimacy, and at first glance it is impossible to state that they are suited, as is, to peoples of various cultures.

A look at the administrative area will make the problem more concrete. If we go back far enough, we find that all Western administrations derive from French practices. It was the Norman, then the Anjou, administrations which crossed into England, and thence to the various English-speaking countries. It was the Burgundy administration that moved into the Low Countries (today the Benelux nations) and then, by the marriage of Marie de Bourgogne, into Austria and Spain. Louis XVI's administration was imitated by Prussia, and we all know to what extent the Napoleonic administrative methods influenced the various nations of Europe. Whether the influence derives from a more or less ancient wave, such as the Norman or Burgundian, or is of more recent vintage, as with the Napoleonic wave, they adjust to and are enriched by the various places where they have been introduced. Governments have everywhere striven to increase the efficiency of their administrative methods and strengthen their claim to legitimacy by adjusting to the mores, traditions, and temperament of their people. The guarantees given the people against administrative despotism have varied with the character traits of different peoples and their historical evolution. In France, for instance, these guarantees consist mainly of the sheer weight of bureaucratic rules which restrict the administrators' freedom of action; in the United States, of the relatively important role played by local authorities and by the power of the judiciary. These features are quite as important as the constitutional organization, which in practice never quite conforms to theory.

All the political-administrative systems presently operative in the West are not machines which can be exactly reproduced by using them as scale models, but are rather living organisms created and shaped by circumstances. There was nothing surprising about the failure of the fantastic project formulated by the French Revolution to reproduce a Sparta distorted by the legend of the Roman Republic, but it is even more remarkable that the Montesquieu-inspired attempt to reproduce the English system resulted in nothing but failure. Then too, the states of Latin America have not really managed to reproduce the North American constitutional democracy with any real measure of success. However well economic methods may be transferred intact, political systems can only be transplanted with great difficulty, which is hardly surprising given their moral content.

It is obvious that a system based solely on efficiency is vastly superior, at least over the short term, to systems imbued with legitimacy. The conflict between Napoleon and Europe proved this beyond all doubt. And by "legitimacy" I do not at all mean the invocation of a simple principle, but the adaptation to the customs and feelings of the people.

As a result, the leaders of new states, who find themselves faced with enormous tasks, are constantly tempted to construct systems based on efficiency. Quite naturally they encounter the opposition of traditional feeling exemplified by the traditional authorities. We Westerners would like to see a "constitutional center" emerge between an "authoritarian left" and a "traditionalist right"; but it seems to me that it would be wrong for us to hold off recognizing this "center" as such until it has

reached legitimacy according to our standards: if it is to succeed it must satisfy local standards. Once again then, the legitimacy of a procedure is not determined by its likeness to a given
model, but by its acceptance by those who use it. A legitimate
procedure can be recognized by the fact that it meets with the
least amount of effective resistance. Our procedures have been
modeled by following the lines of least psychological resistance
in our respective countries. The same is true for the new states.
The more we try to recommend our forms and procedures, the
more it will appear as if we are offering obstacles to efficiency,
which the particular situation does not justify.

I have paused to discuss the new states because their development is of passionate interest to all of us—it is certainly the
most important phenomenon of the contemporary world. Let
me come back to the West. As I have already said, the slogan
of efficacity which prevails with us in the area of economics
colors our judgments and makes us impatient about the delays
and weightiness of public procedures. I am sure there is not
one among us who, when his favorite project is at stake, would
not gladly choose a structure of power whose efficacity would
enable his pet reform to be quickly accomplished, but this structure must serve only this one project and last only long enough
to see it completed. But we know that such will never be the
case, and that the slow, ponderous procedures which keep us
from imposing what we believe to be salutary also protect us
against what we would find odious.

According to our concepts and ways of thinking, it is not
necessarily good to impose something which might of itself be
good. Take for instance the conflicts in the American steel mills:
it is doubtless true that shop methods are an obstacle to improved productivity, and that productivity is desirable. But does
it therefore necessarily follow that management should have a
free hand in modifying shop methods whenever it so desires? Is
it difficult to understand the workers' attachment to that clause
of the collective contract which protects these set routines; for

although this clause is an obstacle to increased productivity, at the same time it protects the methods dear to the workers. This leads us to define what a legitimate method really is: it is one which has a sufficient respect *of* feelings so that what results from it is respected *by* feelings.

But a person who is more and more concerned with better results is also ever less tolerant of methods which imply circumspection and delay. And since, moreover, our political regimes legitimatize political competition, and since the race for victory calls for the most efficient methods, the concern for efficiency thus finds its way into politics. And if it is all right to employ the most efficient methods in winning political power, why not use them in the exercise of that power? There is reason to wonder whether the reassuring ritualism of legitimate procedures in politics can be maintained in those societies where the notion of efficiency is all-important.

I would like to make a few remarks about war, since they are pertinent to my subject, and especially because they might induce Mr. Andrzejewski, who has written a major work on the connection between the military and the political organizations, to say a few words. The art of war is geared solely to one objective, namely, the defeat of the enemy, so that the aggressor can impose his will. Since it has a simple, clearly defined goal, military science naturally is subject to the general law of action, the principle of economy. It is a matter of attaining the objective with a minimum of means.

Thus it is a serious error to call a war conducted with the aid of science's terrifying resources—"scientific warfare." We would not call a pilot "scientific" because he caused grave destruction using a machine which represents the last word in scientific development. War cannot, and should not, be called "scientific" unless it achieves its goal with a minimum of expenditure. The peak of "scientific warfare" was attained in the eighteenth century (or, to be more precise, at the end of the seventeenth and beginning of the eighteenth) when a great general was deemed to be the one who, without engaging in battle, made the enemy retreat. The superstition of battle was introduced by the generals of the French Revolution, because they had at their disposal the "cannon fodder" resulting from conscription, which had been an innovation of the Revolution. Under the old regime, the soldier had been an expensive item, and consequently been treated with deference; with compulsory military service, he became "free"; as a result, the military technique of "the line" was replaced by the concept of "the column" which Folard had advocated as early as 1723, but which had not been practiced until the Revolution because it was considered the path to slaughter. Two factors were thus responsible for France's winning so many victories: numerical superiority and a disdain for man.

The intellectual—and moral—decadence in the art of war reached its culmination with World Wars I and II, in which means you all know were used to achieve the results we see today. At this stage, war was conceived of as solely and uniquely a battle, that is, the exact opposite of what war should be according to the ideas of the eighteenth century.

In the light of this brief historical sketch of what war means and is, we have in recent times witnessed a new development which we owe to the communists. One can compel a country to detach itself from a coalition by crushing it with armed might; this Napoleon did with Prussia in 1806, to take a recent example. But it is also possible to achieve the same result by the internal subversion of the same country. To go back a little in history, the Prince of Orange handled the Anglo-French coalition by getting rid of England via the "glorious revolution." He managed this by his open and personal involvement. But this is not essential: Iraq quit the Baghdad Pact without its being possible to establish any link between its withdrawal and Russian intervention.

Fortunately, I do not believe that the massive arms of destruction stockpiled by the major powers necessarily have to be used. But it is quite possible that the "atomic peace," and even the immobility of conventional armies, can assume the form of conflict in which a coalition would lose its members one by one by successive "political coups." All it takes are well-trained political teams versed in the art of "political techniques," which are increasingly effective. American control of the Panama Canal may be lost as the result of a naval battle; it can also be lost through a political maneuver.

What I have been saying here about war may seem like a digression, but perhaps it will not seem so if you stop to realize that today it is becoming clear that an "economic" reduction of war to "subversive action" injects the element of "efficient methods"—divorced from any semblance of legitimacy—into the realm of politics.

I hope I have made myself clear as to what I am chiefly concerned about here. Politics is the area of conflicting values, and any problem which does not imply such a conflict is simply "technical" and can be solved by "experts." But any problem which does embody such a conflict is not subject to solution and requires a settlement which can only be rendered "respectable" insofar as there is respect for the methods used. Yet, in politics, whenever men set themselves a single goal, such as the conquest of power, their limited criterion subjects their actions to the general maxim of "efficiency," and they have to choose the most efficient methods, completely ignoring the legitimacy of procedures. Similarly, once they have come to power, if they measure the scope of their task solely in terms of a single orientation —such as the progress of this or that basic item of production— once again their actions will be guided by the notion of efficiency.

You can see what I am afraid of, namely, that the slogan of "efficiency" does away with legitimate methods. In the struggle for power, the practical advantage lies with the team or party concerned solely with efficiency in the conquest of power. Similarly, on a short-term basis (and short-term can mean thirty, forty, or fifty years) a government whose sole criterion is "efficiency" can enjoy a great advantage over a government burdened by lawful and sanctioned methods. I am sure the merits of these lawful, legitimate methods will always be rediscovered. But we can picture a sort of chain reaction in which various peoples are successively seduced by political expediency, while those who had been the first to utilize it revert progressively to legitimate methods. But the tendency toward this "return" will be offset by the competitive menace of those peoples still in a state of "efficacious" effervescence. I am terrified by "efficaciousness" in politics, which to my mind corresponds to a basic error as to the nature of politics, which never consists of striving toward a single goal or advancing only in one direction.

By nature, politics is something extremely complex, which cannot be reduced to a simple definition and for which the technique of efficiency is poorly suited; not only does it require complex methods, but in part it is these methods. The same attitudes that produce excellent results in industry may be extremely dangerous in politics. It is imperative that we restore legitimate methods to their rightful position.

LINDBLOM: In my opinion the distinction between the political and economic questions and processes may lead to somewhat paradoxical conclusions. Let me take two examples other than war. In Russia, it is easy to see that, in spite of the distinction made between economics and politics, the latter is wholly subordinate to the former. The state quite simply becomes an enormous factory, and consequently the leaders treat the population as factors of production. This development is conceivable for any state, not only Russia. Paradoxically, the distinction becomes pointless, but the fact that politics has become wholly subordinate to economics remains. There are no variations of judgments, or opinions, or ends; there are no other ends except those ascribed to Marx.

The second example is the United States. If we think of economic matters as the product of highly specialized institutions able to act by creating the minimum of conflicts of value and the minimum number of objectives, we see that even in the United States the workers' demands in the areas of management participation, better working conditions, or the establishment of a system of arbitration to settle management-labor disputes are increasingly a mixture of political and economic methods and considerations, and the role of the state in what seem to be specialized economic processes is constantly growing.

The distinction is once again dubious, although one can always allege that a purely economic aspect can be isolated from a political-economic context. And yet it is practically impossible at the present time to detect one of these aspects, and I'm afraid that in the future this will be more and more the case.

ARON: It seems to me we would clarify the discussion if we asked Bertrand de Jouvenel whether he excludes the maximization of the result from politics because it implies a multiplicity of objectives so that it is impossible to maximize one of the desired results without diminishing the others, or does he think that the very essence of politics is such as to exclude the whole quantitative notion of maximizing, even for a specific objective? A second question implied by what Professor Lindblom said is this: does he or does he not think the nature of politics is such as to prevent a maximization in the economic sector? The first question seems to me fundamental. From what you said, I think we can conceive of the maximization of a result, but this inevitably implies the reduction of one of the other objectives that ought to be pursued.

JOUVENEL: Where there are several judges and several frames of reference, a positive value for one may be negative for another whenever there are differences of opinion. This is the essence of the political problem. I expressed myself poorly when I said that because there are several objectives it is impossible to maximize.

Whether or not the very nature of the political apparatus stands in the way of maximizing in the area of economics, as Professor Lindblom wondered, is an extremely important question, and obviously a major one in the choice of political regimes.

In my opinion, when power is in the hands of a unified, harmonious team—which, by definition, presupposes a single system of values—and when economic progress is considered to consist of a certain specific rate of growth, then this government, this harmonious "team" can, by pursuing clearly defined goals, very well attain them. The basic difference between the Soviet and American economies is this: if you take the per capita output of steel as a criterion for success, you take it *ex post* in the case of the United States and *ex ante* in the case of Russia. Then you say that the Americans have reached this stage of development with such and such per capita consumption of steel. Now, we are going to attain the same stage by equaling their per capita consumption. But this is false reasoning, because in one case the per capita consumption is a sign and in the other it has become a goal. This is the essential difference between the two types of economies.

LINDBLOM: I am not sure I understand the difference, but I believe you are setting up various distinctions between economic phenomena and political phenomena. On the one hand, you maintain that our economic processes are maximizing processes while our political processes are not, and that at least in certain cases they are, on the contrary, processes for resolving conflicts aimed at solutions which will cause the minimum amount of damage. It is obviously possible to think of many various processes not generally classified as typically maximizing; for instance, we can consider the methods for reaching settlements with the minimum amount of harm or damage as processes which tend to maximize social peace or harmony, however we define it. Thus it is quite possible that the distinction between economics as a maximizing process and politics considered as a nonmaximizing process simply reflects a habit that we have adopted when we reconstruct these processes intellectually, rather than a real, basic difference. I therefore believe this argument is less important than certain other distinctions.

Perhaps I ought to ask a question. Since these differences between the characteristics of the economic and political processes do exist, to what extent do you maintain that the latter are ineffective in stimulating or activating the former? I was not clear on this point, which seems to me of prime importance in your paper. Could you clarify this for me before I go on?

JOUVENEL: I had no intention of going into this question. I do not see why public authorities, faced with a technical problem, would not act like any private authority. I do not think this is what defines government.

LINDBLOM: If I asked that question it was because I understood from my discussion yesterday with Mr. de Jouvenel that his thesis is as follows: since these clear-cut differences do exist, perhaps we can predict that, with the exception of a short period of time when the political processes will benefit from a certain initial enthusiasm, over the long term they are incapable of an effective maximizing action. From this you draw the following conclusion: we can foresee that the Soviet system will be successful for a while and will inspire a certain number of successful imitations throughout the world. But in the end—to pursue your reasoning—the Soviet political organization and its foreign imitations will be less successful than the systems of economic organization which, by the interplay of supply and demand or other means, give rise to nongovernmental, specialized techniques capable of carrying production to maximum levels. This fact did not emerge clearly from our discussion; perhaps you preferred not to deal with the question, but in my opinion the idea is extremely interesting.

TALMON: It seems to me that certain questions raised by Mr. de Jouvenel are related to the problems we have already discussed, such as those of ideology, economy, and politics. Let me first of all clarify what I am going to say by offering a few concrete examples. At the present time in the West we hear the pessimists saying that the Soviet experiment has proved itself so conducive to rapid industrialization and produced such spectacular results in the technical sphere that the non-European countries and civilizations of Asia and the rest of the world which are unused to democratic procedures, persuasions, institutions, etc., will obviously be tempted to follow the Soviet example and come to the conclusion that only the nonpluralistic procedures are effective for rapid industrialization. Admittedly, this type of argument is not completely unconvincing. As has already been said before, how can hundreds of millions of Chinese or Indians who for centuries have lived in degrading misery be concerned about democracy or democratic methods? What they want is bread and other basic necessities of life.

Now, the question I ask myself is this: we always hear about the contradiction between the uselessness and absence of goals characteristic of politics and the usefulness of economics and industrialization—on the one hand, the mobilization of all resources, possessions, and talents to achieve a certain result; on the other, the lack of any goal in politics, which is only looking to maintain or re-establish an equilibrium, give certain guarantees, etc. In reality the question is this—and here I arrive at what is perhaps the underlying hypothesis on which Mr. Aron's report is based: does this concern of our society over the pursuit of a goal really derive, in the final analysis, from economics, or rather from politics? I am inclined to believe that it stems from politics, and perhaps because I presuppose it, from the ideological sphere.

After the Russian Revolution, the Soviet Union did not make industrialization its objective. Its goal was an ideological one. As we all know, the industrialization of Russia was not aimed—at least immediately—at the production of consumer goods, but at strengthening the military in order to render Russia invulnerable in case of war. It was from this effort that the conditions were created which now enable the increased production of consumer goods.

My contention is that we are victims of an optical illusion.

We now have the impression that this concern—I might even say obsession—with and straining toward an objective stem from a certain experience of economic development. But such is not the case; in fact, the very opposite has taken place. Everything began with politics, and only later did economic growth came to the fore. By that I mean that the objective of maximum production has become an end in itself and politics has been forgotten. But it all started with politics. In fact, the phenomenon is an extremely ancient one. As early as the beginning of the seventeenth century, Francis Bacon grudgingly made the following observations, in these extremely interesting lines: "It is regrettable—and the origin of all evil—that considerations of wealth have given way to considerations of power." Here is the problem in a nutshell. And throughout history, as Mr. de Jouvenel pointed out in his paper and Mr. Andrzejewski in his book, war has been the great ferment of rationalization. How paradoxical that the most futile, most irrational thing in the world has been the great cause of rationalization, for military preparation implies planning, mobilization of resources, rationalization. In this respect, the pre-eminence of politics in modern societies signifies the pre-eminence of war, but at the present time the lessening of political tension and the relaxation of the ideological war seem to suggest that the historical order is reversed.

Conclusion

ARON: The problem we set ourselves, that of political institutions, was approached from different levels. Mr. Kennan dealt with it from the standpoint of representative institutions. Mr. Mehta and several other speakers made a distinction between the democratic idea or ideas and the specific institutions of such and such a Western country. We tried to ascertain to what extent democratic ideas could be satisfied without taking over the exact institutional forms which these ideas have assumed in various Western countries. There was also a much more abstract plane of discussion, with Mr. de Jouvenel trying to define the difference between economics and politics, which perhaps boils down to the opposition between technique, which deals with the application of efficient means tending toward a specific goal, and politics, where the problem is one of perfecting certain procedures in order to arrive at decisions. Actually, I was tempted to conclude that the distinction he was making is roughly the distinction between the ways of doing or producing and ways of living. Finally, politics does not strike me as the means to an end; it is an end in itself. It defines a certain way of living together, and this is why procedure, as opposed to technique, is an integral part of politics.

The third aspect of the discussion had to do with the relationship between politics and economics. We can say that under the Soviet system politics is at the service of the economy because social organization is subordinated to the goal of maximum production; but we can just as easily say, by reversing the proposition, that since the economy is completely state controlled, it is politics which shapes the entire society and therefore politics has top priority. I think that this dialectic is revealing, for it gets to the heart of our problem: since the goal of all these societies is efficient production, we end up posing the problem of politics solely as a means toward the end of maximum efficiency. But then we are forgetting that the purpose of maximum production is *not* an end, but a means toward a "good life" as it relates to a certain political objective.

From this point our political-economic dialogue leads us quite naturally to pose the problem which we will now deal with from various points of view: the meaning of industrial society. An initial aspect is that of "millenarianism." Another term for this might be "secular religion"; Mr. Talmon calls it "Messianism." In any event, it is a movement we have had in the West for several centuries, which in our time has been transformed in two ways: by the political experiment and also by the scientific, technical, or economic experiment. This double experiment, which aims at bringing to complete fruition the good society and the total rationalization of society, will be discussed by Mr. Talmon, who will show how this idea has been debased and abjured by fanaticism. At the same time we will take up again our dialogue with the Soviet Union and the two types of society. But at the same time we shall bear in mind the positive problem: what makes a good society?

Part II

The West and the

Meaning of Industrial Society

CHAPTER I: THE DECLINE OF MESSIANISM?

TALMON: From the French Revolution to the present day, Europe has always known the presence of men, or groups of men, who were ardently preparing for the Day—with a capital "D"—and whose acts were motivated by the conviction that history was moving inevitably toward a fatal denouement, a predestined goal. These men have kept themselves in readiness for the Day, either as Promethean heros capable of modifying reality or as the midwives of History, with a capital "H." Their movements have constituted an entity which has an identity and continuity and which I shall call the cause of the Revolution or the Messianic movement. The Bolshevik Revolution appeared as the culmination of this movement. Actually, there is reason to wonder whether this sort of ideological abatement, this lessening of ideological tension which we see taking place throughout the world is not an indication that the Messianic movement, born a century and a half ago, is not on the wane, and whether we shouldn't expect some new development. What to me is most striking is that this political Messianism, born and nurtured in Western Europe, was fated not to triumph in Western Europe but to spread toward the East, develop in Russia, and thence push on to the Far East, eventually reaching other continents. What will become of this political Messianism transplanted into a completely new civilization? I can only say that in the case of religion the fact of moving from its birthplace—from the

163

nation which engendered but refused to accept it—to a wholly new civilization where it takes root, is not without precedent in history. Was this not the fate of both Christianity and Buddhism?

What then is the content of political Messianism? The chief characteristics of Messianic thinkers and theologians—from Rousseau to Marx and including Saint-Simon, Fourier, and the others—is that each feels absolutely compelled to initiate and pursue his research by settling accounts with religion. All of them are completely—and I might even say intensely and aggressively—conscious that they are offering a substitute for religion. The appearance of political Messianism at the end of the eighteenth century coincides with the decline of religion as a power and force of social cohesion. Political Messianism is characterized by its deep-seated desire for unity, its meditations on the problem and mystery of the one and the many. We find ourselves in the presence of a rational, scientific *élan* and at the same time, as Professor Postan was mentioning to me, an ultra-rational movement which, consequently, becomes irrational. It is ultrarational or ultrascientific in that it believes it can completely become pantheistic and immediately embrace everything instead of moving empirically from one thing to another, adding discoveries to verifications.

The task of political Messianism is to combine two contradictory things within a single reality: the desire of self-expression and the need for social cohesion. Beyond political Messianism, we find the necessity to resolve the contradictions which characterize society and are the curse of history. Here the attack on religion and Christianity assumes the form of a debate on the ideas of man's fall from grace and original sin. The contrast between human imperfection and divine omnipotence implies that man will never be able to save himself through his own efforts and needs grace. Whence his readiness, by hate or self-disdain, to acquiesce to any sort of tyranny and exploitation, because he deserves no better.

The solution of political Messianism is drastic; it already existed in the eighteenth century. Man's shortcomings, so it goes, are not in the least inherent but derive from defective and vicious institutions which are themselves based on the notion of original sin. All evil comes from frustration. If free expression were granted to human needs, they would arrange themselves in a harmonious model of social cohesion and order. This conviction is, by its very essence, one of the manifestations of the greed of Western civilizations, both Judaic and Roman. It's a question of the compelling necessity not to be satisfied with the *hic et nunc.* At its inception, political Messianism is imbued with an exaggerated faith in human nature and its ability to adapt, and in the rationality of both man and society. Since the disciples of Messianism are convinced that man is predestined to attain perfection, they see themselves not as the instruments of constraint but as the representatives of history, not as tyrants but as midwives. The often forceful and rigorous means used are educational techniques whose purpose is to hasten the progress of the slow, the lazy, the unimaginative, etc. Once the final solution has been created, it is thought that these laggards will understand that this is what they always wanted and intended to do. The tyrannical aspect of Messianic totalitarian regimes offers an example of the worst resulting from the erosion of the best. It is the noble dissatisfaction with the real which evolves into intransigent *ubris,* arrogance, and pride. There were of course earlier Messianic movements of a religious nature. But the basic difference seems to be this: in the periods when faith still prevailed, the millennial sects were animated by a holy impatience, but they were nonetheless certain that the final reckoning was never on earth but somewhere else, a notion based on the fallibility of flesh and blood. In a way, these convictions prevented the advent of fanatical terrorism which has been the mark of modern political Messianism, which is impregnated with impatience, anxious to get things settled *hic et nunc,* since beyond there is nothing. Once the sense of destiny becomes so overwhelming and the stakes so high, the justification for using force becomes subjectively so intense that moral sensitivity becomes deadened to it. Through a mixture of exaggerated sadism, a persistent striving for power, and objective idealism, one ends up deceiving oneself. In our time this mixture has become frighteningly dangerous because—and this is the most important event of the age—technology has put into the hands of the Messianic leaders terrifying means for carrying out their designs. Political Messianism really assumes apocalyptic proportions. The yearning to take a step toward eternal happiness, toward pure reason and triumphant rationality runs afoul of the danger of global suicide.

A quick glance back will show that in the eighteenth century Rousseau and the French revolutionaries were faced with the problem in the following terms: they wanted to be both free and equal. How could they be free, that is, free to express themselves, and at the same time equal, that is, submitting to the common level required by an egalitarian society? There was only one solution: the belief that eventually men could reach unanimity, and the notion of a unanimous auto-identification with the general will.

The French Revolution coincided with another major revolution—the Industrial Revolution. In the midst of uncertainties and imponderables, the scientific principle was made incarnate by the Industrial Revolution and seemed the path to salvation. The demands of industrial organization and the precepts of the division of labor meant that it was actually possible to put into effect the yearning for freedom of expression and social cohesion. Thus it was that a sort of marriage or synthesis took place between what I shall call Messianic political movement and faith in the Messianic possibilities of industry, industrial organization, and industrial development. This search for a synthesis between individual expression and social cohesion—a synthesis to be achieved through the Industrial Revolution—ran afoul of private property, the main stumbling block in the way of using over-all planning to harmonize social advantages and human talents. This is why the abolition of private property became the prime concern of all Messianic thinkers during the first half of the nineteenth century and beyond.

In 1848, political Messianism went through a crisis. It discovered that its principal opponent was not political democracy or liberalism, but nationalism. During the first half of the nineteenth century, the socialist and nationalist versions of political Messianism were thought to be one and the same, or at least complementary, because they were fighting a common enemy —the dynastic governments of Europe. In the second half of the nineteenth century, when political Messianism in the West seemed to have passed its peak and to be on the wane, nationalism offered a substitute for the desires and aspirations which had formerly served to inspire the revolutionary camp. The nation *per se* offered a tangible substitute for such ethereal and abstract confraternities as "mankind," "the international proletariat," "the evolution of the working class," etc. Nationalism offered the individual a chance to express himself and also gave him a focus of loyalty—sometimes fanatic loyalty. As a result, during this period from 1850–1900, Messianism acquired this curious trait which it has retained to the present day: It engendered a kind of bastard socialism, a bastard Messianism which in recent times has found expression in Fascist movements.

On this subject, anti-Semitic movements have become a universally important *exécutoire* because they offer the possibility of uniting the two currents of political Messianism: social resentment and nationalistic frustration. This kind of nationalism has modified the character of politcal Messianism, which has evolved from a religion into a neurosis: forsaking the concepts of universal justice and the inherent value of man (which is basically a religious trait), it is reduced to the claim of grandeur for the ethnic or national entity, its power and fulfillment, and ceases to be rational.

At the present time—and this is the new ambivalence of nationalism in our era—nationalism has become a guide in the antitotalitarian defense of freedom. (I think of phenomena such as Hungary and Poland.) The conviction that harmonious, rational plans can be imposed upon humanity, the importance of proselytism in any universal ideology, encounter resistance from things which are, which exist, for no other reason except they are present: history, geography, individuality, human perversity. On this score, in our time nationalism is the affirmation of individualism and freedom of expression, of concrete individuality in the presence of abstract, universal, and coercive organizations.

I shall come full circle and conclude where I began. It is entirely possible that political Messianism has ceased to be a dynamic, living reality, but it has spread eastward, to Russia and the Far East. I shall confine myself to asking questions which my ignorance prevents me from answering. As I have already noted, European political Messianism was in a sense the expression of a guilt complex, a feeling of suffering and obsessive preoccupation with the legitimacy of power. We are told—and this is true to a point, but in the case of Russia only to a point—that in the history of Far Eastern civilizations this prophetic concern with the legitimacy of power is nonexistent. In other words, power is considered as a natural phenomenon— at times beneficent, at times maleficent—but always descended from heaven, no doubt because these civilizations did not immediately conceive of man as a political creature but as someone in contact with cosmic forces. This conception leads not only to the acceptance of any authority whatsoever—since in any event one is powerless to do anything about it—but also to the absence of what has distinguished Europe through the centuries: various nuclei of autonomous governments, efforts to co-operate, a collective purpose or will. We have seen that political Messianism, or at least its nineteenth-century version, combines these two postulates: the desire for self-expression and the desire for organization or cohesion. This being the case, I cannot help wondering what will become of political Messianism in these Far Eastern civilizations for whom the legitimacy of power has never been a concern. Will they not be reduced to adopting the organizational aspect of political Messianism, a kind of instrument for constructing enormous power machines, and to renouncing its prophetic mission? If so, and if we recall that in the end nationalistic traits or peculiarities have shown themselves to be much more powerful and infinitely stronger than Messianic universalism, is it not to be feared that if these Oriental civilizations do disregard the prophetic tradition and adopt a kind of "organizational Messianism" they will turn Messianism into a tool with which to forge the instruments of power destined to support what is unique and different about them and also to thwart Western civilization, which has been guilty of so many past oppressions.

My second conclusion is that, contrary to nineteenth-century thought, the further scientific rationality progressed, the more man's irrationality and inadaptability became apparent; the spread of rationality renders man impotent—perhaps only temporarily—to deal with it, classify it, or control it. Never before has man had such extraordinary opportunities, and yet never has his feeling of impotence and resignation been greater. And it is paradoxical that because of this prodigious scientific and industrial rationalization the great and fatal decisions which affect all of us are made by a handful of men. By placing tremendous technical means for suicide in the hands of these men, scientific rationalization has posed a threat to human freedom far exceeding anything the past has ever seen. For nineteenth-century man, Messianism represented either a Promethean movement or a certain way of shunning his responsibilities. He hoped that history, the laws of necessity, and the demands of an industrial civilization would free him from the necessity of making decisions. But the Kantian lesson to be derived from the evolution of Messianism takes the form of a challenge: as rationality —collective rationality—grows and spreads, the need for moral autonomy, and for unrestrained decision-making, becomes increasingly important.

VOEGELIN: I would like to cite a few historical examples as a reminder that the problem we are dealing with is not specifically a modern one, but a general human problem which in one form or another has existed throughout history.

The origins of what Professor Talmon calls "Messianism"

obviously go back to Israel. We can in fact situate them fairly closely in a political event which took place eight centuries before Christ. At the time of the siege of Jerusalem by the Aramaeans, who were allies of the Israelites, the prophet Isaiah came to the king and asked him not to take up arms but to disarm and put his trust in God, believing that, with His help, their enemies would destroy each other or be decimated by an epidemic. Here we have the model or prototype of the disarmament concept: if you put your trust in nature, not as it is but as it will one day be, if you really do believe, then all the annoyances or unpleasantness of politics, including the necessity to resort to arms, will vanish.

This sort of faith calls for a new term. I have provisionally proposed the term "metastasis." By this I mean an attitude on the part of the person who believes that through an act of faith —or any other act—human nature will cease to be what it is and, in one way or another, will be replaced by a new transfigured human nature, a new society, and a new transfigured history. Nineteenth-century political Messianism belongs to this type of metastatic belief.

The various historical types of metastasis, which begin with the history of Judaism, can roughly be broken down into two stages. The first opens after the exile, in apocalyptic times, when apocalyptic symbols were used to portray the coming of paradise on earth. These symbols passed over into Christianity through the revelations of Saint John, chapters 21 and 22, and are the sources of subsequent credos of this sort, particularly those at the basis of the "Puritan Revolution." Apocalyptic symbolism came to an end about the beginning of the eighteenth century, after the Puritan Revolution when the transcendental faith sustaining apocalyptic symbolism was replaced by what we shall call secularism or "immanentism." We then find ourselves confronted with a new kind of Messianism, which no longer utilizes the old apocalyptic symbols but instead employs that sort of symbolism which in the nineteenth century was termed "the philosophy of history." The philosophy of history—

as Condorcet, Comte, Hegel, and Marx understood it—is that school of thought which replaced the old apocalyptic symbolism. In order to distinguish it from the earlier form, we should perhaps speak of a secular or "immanentist" symbolism.

The quest for another constituent element of this Messianism compels me to raise the problem of "gnosis," which in itself has no direct bearing either on apocalyptic or immanentist symbolism. It originated independently of but at approximately the same time as Christianity, and taught that terrestrial paradise will not come to pass through divine intervention but through man's own efforts. There can be no doubt that the gnostic movement has continued from antiquity down to the present day. We must therefore constantly keep in mind this notion of the redemption of the individual through his own efforts, and his salvation through action. At what times in history do such gnostic movements, based on this idea of immanentist self-redemption, become fanatic and constitute a danger to society?

This intriguing question also takes us back to antiquity. Jeremiah was the first to make the interesting anthropological observation that men remain faithful to their gods as long as they are false gods; it is only when you have the real God, as Israel had, that you betray him. Translated into modern terms, this is the same as saying that when one's spiritual and intellectual life has reached a certain degree of differentiation one is struck by the uncertainty of the transcendental relationship. Most people find this unbearable, and seek to replace the uncertainty of truth by the certitude of error. This is a general phenomenon in society—it was at the core of the Platonic and Aristotelian conceptions of politics. Both these philosophers realistically admit that for most people the philosophic life, which they consider man's real life, is inaccessible. This is why their conceptions, including all the Platonic designs, are always based on the premise of a philosophic ruling class, and the recognition that there is nothing one can do about the masses, who will never attain the philosophic level of existence. This is an admission of fact. We can verify it empirically by noting that this is true for Greece, in the history of Israel, and again in the twelfth century of our Western civilization, at the time of the great spiritual ferment of the cities and, in the religious orders, when there began the elaboration of immanentist theories according to which there will be a third kingdom of the spirit within history which the Paraclete will introduce. Here we see the contribution—if we can call it that—of Joachim de Flore. This descent into immanentism begins at the height of the spirituality of the Middle Ages, and has one curious political repercussion, for the history of Christianity reveals no original political theory. In the early days of Christianity, the notion prevailed that politics was the province of the Roman Empire. The problem of political theory arose only when that Empire was visibly beginning to crumble in the Middle Ages and new types of communities—national states—were slowly beginning to emerge. It then became necessary to evolve a theory for this new type of society which was bound neither to the Empire nor to the Church. In its modern form, political theory thus begins roughly in the middle of the fifteenth century: its real beginning—and this is a highly significant fact—is in Fortescue's *Government of England*. In answering the question "What are the people?" the Christian notion of *corpus mysticum* is transferred to England as a nation, which is then a *corpus mysticum* in need of a kind of organization.

This proves that, apart from transcendental religiousness in the Christian sense, man also yearns for an explanation of his social existence, of his "community" in immanentist terms. There is also a technical term for this need, which goes back to antiquity, to Varro and Cicero, who refer to it as the desire for a *theologia civilis*. Besides a natural and supernatural theology, people need a civil theology. Throughout the political history of the West, the movements which Mr. Talmon referred to aimed at supplying the masses with a civil theology, otherwise lacking. This enormous social pressure which the need for a civil theology engenders is an emotional pressure strong enough to sustain any ideology. From all this we can draw the following conclusion: wherever civil theology arose during a profoundly Christian era, such as in England and subsequently in America, the notion of the "civil government," which is the institutional translation of the vestiges of classical and Christian tradition, prevails. In these places, false ideologies have less of a chance to flourish and seem less enticing than in the countries which have never known such institutions, such as those of Central Europe, which will be much more vulnerable to an ideology than, say, England or America.

These historical phenomena must be taken seriously. I do not share Mr. Kennan's views when he declares that all will be well in Russia when the young people will no longer be taken in by an ideology which is patently worthless. Russian youth is like youth anywhere: it aspires to some form or other of civil theology, and if it rejects communism—which seems possible—I hate to think what it may espouse in its place. Nothing says that Russian youth will simply revert to "rational theologies," to the "life of reason." Whenever one ideology is abandoned and there is nothing to replace it, when there is no civil theology for the people, we can expect the worst. This is why I wanted to emphasize the historical aspects of the problem.

DEL CORRAL: There is no doubt that Messianism tends toward extremes. But I believe the West has managed to impose a measure of restraint on the Messianic *élan* and other similar phenomena. I submit that what we call typically Western is a kind of hope imbued with a strong sense of the future, but also characterized by calculated and reasonable methods. Otherwise neither the idea of progress nor progress itself would have been able to develop in the Western world. I also think it is worth bearing in mind the notion of and experience with hope in the orthodox, Slavic world. Mr. Talmon has already reminded us that an understanding of Russian communism must begin with the phenomenon of a secularization which is not progressive and differentiated, as in the Western world, but radical, almost instantaneous. This secularization is based on a form which con-

tains a great many more millennial and eschatological elements
than exist in Western Christianity. Since the time of the medieval
Scholastics, Christianity in the West has in a sense been rational-
ized. Dostoevsky's radical hope in the absolute of man has
evolved into a more concrete and material form of hope. To a
certain degree, totalitarianism is the paradoxical result of this
transmutation.

SPERBER: I think that in the same century when Messianism
seemed to have the greatest ascendancy over the mind and
heart of man, as well as over his actions, it was in fact moribund.
Let me explain: Professor Voegelin did not place sufficient emphasis on the eschatological aspect of Messianism. Behind every
Messianic movement there lurks the same question: What is the
meaning of man's passage here on earth? For Isaiah, it was above
all a question of ascertaining whether one could move from time
to eternity, that is, do away with death. For humanity in general
—with the exception of the handful of men who were born
leaders—history was like death: something that happened to
you, not something you could act upon. But these people believe
they can fashion history, that it can be their handiwork. This
reversal from passive to active is highly significant.

   From the standpoint of belief, there is such a fundamental
difference between the communist of today and the communist
of twenty or forty years ago that we would be justified in using
different terms. Who could have foretold the ideological collapse
of the Hungarian Revolution or the October Revolution in
Poland? Who could have guessed how quickly a youth raised
on and apparently formed by a powerful, monolithic ideology
would divest himself of it? In the present century there is an
ideology which has it that men live in ideology. My generation
was perhaps the last avant-garde, that is, in reality the rear
guard. We were the last to try to live an ideology, and we destroyed it. Today, people no longer believe there is any end to
history, a solution to every problem. But they are convinced

that every human being has certain inalienable rights such as dignity, well-being, and a good society—rights which not too long ago were not taken for granted. But in the most remote villages of the world a growing number of men believe today that they, too, have a right to material comfort and their children a right to a better life.

Finally and above all, it is the success of the industrial society which has enabled us to solve the material problems which Marxism rightly stressed, so that we can now turn to the question of the meaning of existence: not "how" to live, but "why" and "for what" we live.

BICANIC: I am primarily interested in one of the problems raised by political Messianism; that is, how it fares with the post-war generation. Also, what does it mean to the present generation, formed between the two World Wars? I shall limit myself to pointing out that the chief worry of many of our contemporaries is that the rising generation, the post-World War II generation, shows no signs of political Messianism. What I find most strange is that this phenomenon appears to exist both in the capitalist and communist countries. I strongly fear that we are here faced with a void which should concern us. Nor should we look only at the negative side of the problem—the points of conflict—but also try to ferret out what is positive about this new generation's preoccupations. And I think there *is* something positive. I believe that today a militant Catholic over forty and a militant communist over forty have much more in common than two militant Catholics, one over forty and the other twenty, or two communists of like ages. Taking my own part of the world—Yugoslavia—I might add there is no Bolshevik Messianism among the youth. Our young people have their own ideas and vision of the future. At present, it is an increasingly negative view. They say what they do not want, but I think they also want certain positive things. They consider as finished the accomplishments of the Messianic myth of past generations. For them, socialism is not the fulfillment of a myth; it is a reality. For them, socialism is part of the established social order, and their ambitions go beyond this.

To come back now to the present generation, we should discuss our own conception of society. First of all, I note that by mid-century the "Welfare State" of the first half of the present century is pretty well worn out. I doubt that any young man is ready to lay down his life for a free pair of glasses. On the other hand, we are impressed by the vast process of rationalization that has taken place in various societies. Former revolutionaries now have to deliver merchandise, prove themselves capable administrators, manage and lead their countries—all of which cannot be accomplished by acts of faith, but only by efficaciousness. It is most interesting to study this phenomenon from the standpoint of economic science, which happens to be my specialty. There are certainly differences of opinion among the economists of the Soviet Union, as there were several years back in Yugoslavia. On one side you have the dogmatic economists, men of a single book, and also those who have to analyze the economy concretely and draw up practical plans of economic policy.

The process of rationalizing the myth of the Revolution is accompanied by two by-products. One is the "bureaucratization" of the revolutionaries, who are increasingly ensconced in the middle class. The thin, young, fanatic revolutionaries parading in the streets have in many cases become middle-aged, fat, and smug in their expense-account cars. Equally interesting is this feeling of frustration that all revolutionaries experience when their dreams are realized. Isn't there an old French saying: "How beautiful was our Republic when the Emperor ruled."

There is another important point about Messianism: the minute you stop believing the revolution will be over tomorrow—and experience proves that it will not—then the question arises: what price revolution? Is the weight to be camouflaged by such and such a form of Messianism and borne by the present generation alone, or will it be spread out between this and the rising generation? This is where we get into the problems of the policy of investment and economic growth. Perhaps it is in this sector that we will again run into the problems of Messianism and the conflict of generations.

SALIN: In my opinion, Messianism—in its Judaic-Christian form—has triumphed from the second century to the present. In recent centuries we have witnessed a secularization of this Messianism. Marxism is nothing more than a retarded form of Judaism and Christianity; this Marxist form of Messianism is deeply rooted in Christianity. It has broken loose from it, but even a son who leaves his parents and the home in which he has been raised is still a member of the family. On this point, we see a major difference between what is happening in the West and in the East. It is obvious the Russians have their own Messianism, but not only has it been westernized by Marx, it has also been industrialized. What we now have are production figures and statistics. Since I believe that Khrushchev and the present generation in Russia fully intend to overtake American production, we can be absolutely certain that for another twenty or thirty years the goals of their materialistic Messianism will still be with them. But what will happen after that? I have no idea. But I do observe that on the other side—our side—even that part of Messianism is conspicuously lacking. And I think that herein lies the difficulty and difference. In the West, Messianism has deserted us (it has deserted the "Labour Movement" and the Marxists themselves), leaving behind a disintegrated society, a youth stripped of real hope, while in the East we see a new society still in the process of formation, a society for which secular Messianism will give at least one generation its chance to build a new, interesting, exemplary world, which will be an object of fascination for all the uncommitted nations.

ARON: I would like to say to Professor Salin that I strongly disagree with him; I am far from convinced that the weakening of millenarianism is the sign of the West's disintegration. For me, it is quite the contrary: I see it as the sign of the integration of a society which can do without ideology. I am tempted to rephrase his proposition: to my mind, the remaining vestiges of Messianism in Russia are a profound source of weakness, for it compels the government to tell the people things they know aren't true. But I do not want to provoke an argument; I simply want to say that the matter is open to discussion, and the problem as to how much a millennial ideology helps integrate or coalesce a society efficiently has been questioned. It is possible, as Professor Salin claims, that a millennial philosophy helps cement a society; one can also make a case for the idea that a society which is free of millenarianism is infinitely more integrated in depth.

HERSCH: I would like to know where the "cow" ends and Messianism begins. I picture the cow as someone who watches what is going on and accepts it without protest, and the Messianist as someone who goes to the extreme limits of the possible and perhaps even beyond, to the impossible. It seems to me that you have all been talking as though it were possible to separate Messianism from what man is and get as a residue a person who, in some of your minds, is "the reasonable being." I detected that most especially in Professor Voegelin's paper. For instance, he said it upsets him greatly to see the young communists forsaking their Messianic ideology for a state of reason, the danger being that they will find something else. But there is always something else. And I really wonder how you picture this non-Messianic man. Because man remains man, not a cow. I submit then that it is not a question of suppressing Messianism, but of looking at it in the proper perspective and recognizing what is valid and useful about it.

SPERBER: Admittedly, we all know that man is a forward-looking creature; it is unthinkable for anyone to go on living without the notion of tomorrow. But there is an obvious difference between the Messianism which says: "Tomorrow things will be better," and one that proclaims: "Tomorrow the world will come to an end."

ARON: Miss Hersch asked whether there was not an intermediate situation or attitude between the "cow" attitude and that of the millenarian. I suspect that all of us here believe there is not only one but several intermediate attitudes. No matter how strongly we were opposed to certain forms of millenarianism, none of us has aspired to revert to passivity or self-satisfaction. Mr. Talmon was the first to say that nothing seemed to him more futile than man's interminable dissatisfaction with his situation. But his very precise definition of Messianism or millenarianism contrasted with many other forms of thought directed toward the future or toward truth. What he analyzed and so roundly condemned were those specific methods of transforming a real objective into an inaccessible one, and conversely, destroying reality in the name of an inaccessible goal.

BICANIC: May I quote a Chinese proverb which clarifies the question? The proverb goes: "It is easier to drag a dragon than to drag a carp."

POLANYI: I wonder whether we should not pay closer attention to the fact that the great upheaval which has occurred in the world is not only the advent of Messianism, but also the appearance of a progressive-minded, democratic, reform-oriented society. I would tend to think that a distinction has to be made between the ancient, immemorial, static societies on the one hand and dynamic societies on the other. The former, as Mr. Talmon pointed out, developed with only sporadic explosions of Messianism, and remained basically oriented by a notion of human existence based on continuity; nor did they effectively and concretely direct their hopes toward the future in the secular realm. The "dynamic" societies would include those reformist societies of the nineteenth century, the Messianic movements, and also the totalitarian societies of our time. Static societies nourish no desire to change society radically and work toward the coming of social perfection. Confronting them are two kinds of societies which appear successively: the progressive society and the totalitarian state. Both set themselves an identical political objective: the continuing perfection of society. The obvious difference between them is that the progressive society aims at reaching this goal by slow stages whereas the totalitarian society resorts to revolutionary means to attain the same end in a more ambitious and absolute way. The point of conflict between these two societies is their attitude toward the nature of man, the nature of truth, their notions of the meaning of human charity, honesty, etc. A progressive society has no reason to mistrust these ideas, because it continually takes into account various manifestations which it considers to be authentic factors for the improvement of society. A totalitarian society is influenced much more by science as a guide to reality and the Messianic goals. I therefore believe that its relations with the sphere of ideas are fundamentally reversed. The deep-seated aspirations it shares with progressive society are embodied in a global plan which in principle should correspond with the latest reality as defined by science. Revolutionary societies are highly suspicious, from a philosophical standpoint, of the forces which sustain reformist societies. They do, however, have complete confidence in the material forces of man, in violence, in the fulfillment of appetites, in the unremitting struggle. Let us not forget, however, that the greatest conquests of our secular age have been made by the reformist movements. As far as I can tell, there is absolutely no reason why we should reject the possibility that modern fanatic societies—and the corruption they entail—will not be replaced by a reformist society. All I see standing in the way—and this is admittedly a big obstacle—is the fact that the only confidence we have in reality is that sanctioned by a scientific outlook.

ARON: We began with the major role Messianism played in the political history of our times. Mr. Talmon discussed this transformation of politics by millenarianism from the Messianic point of view and also compared it with English conservatism. The discussion then ranged in various directions: Professor Voegelin gave an interesting historical digest of the origins and evolution of political Messianism; Messrs. Bicanic and Manès Sperber talked of the relative *embourgeoisement*—or comfort seeking— of the revolutionaries of yesterday, both in thought and practice. Then there was my all too brief debate with Professor Salin: there I suspect we were both wrong. He bluntly declared that societies which were losing their political Messianism, or their ideology, were threatened with disintegration, and my reply, which was equally unjust, claimed that societies became more coherent when they lost their ideologies. I believe we both went so far, in opposite directions, that it would have been well worth while pursuing this discussion, which is extremely important. Indeed, one of the key problems of our debate is trying to determine what kind of political system societies need and also whether the decline of Messianic fervor can lead to a world-wide relaxation of tensions comparable to what we have witnessed on a national scale.

I think that Professor Polanyi, with assistance from Miss Hersch, supplied the best answer to our discussion by reminding us that a constant dissatisfaction with reality is an essential part of the human condition: if man *were* satisfied with what he had, he would cease to be man. But Mr. Polanyi hastened to add that there are many kinds of discontent: the dissatisfaction which seeks expression through the search to improve and advance is fertile; that which expresses itself in a total ideology which becomes totalitarian is the origin of intolerance and the wars of religion.

The idea of these two types of discontent leading to two types of societies is an excellent point of departure for the final portion of our discussion, which we shall devote to the search for positive answers.

CHAPTER II: RENAISSANCE OF PHILOSOPHY?

SECTION A—INDUSTRIAL SOCIETY AND "THE GOOD LIFE"

KENNAN: I come now to the questions which Aron has raised in the last portion of his paper and which relate, if I understand them correctly, to the adequacy of the ideological principles, explicit or implicit, by which Western society is today informed.

These questions—concerning the lack of purpose, the lack of any answer as to the uses of leisure, and the shrinking field of politics itself in a satiated world—seem to me very reasonable and well put. But do they, I wonder, go far enough? Are not there other questions, also, that must be raised?

It seems to me that there are certain effects of the modern industrial society which, if not corrected in good time, could well cancel out many of its advantages, and which are nevertheless in no way recognized either in contemporary Western thought or in communist doctrine, and of which I see no recognition in Aron's paper. One of these is overpopulation, and I shall say only that I am thinking here not just of the relation of population to food supply but also of the spiritual effects of overcrowdedness: the lack of privacy, the pervasive urbanization of life, the difficulty of contact and communion with nature.

A second is the reckless, wasteful, and destructive attitude of modern industrial man toward the very natural environment by which and from which he exists: his ruthless, greedy exhaustion of its available resources, his readiness to pollute it almost indefinitely with his human and industrial wastes, of which the by-products of atomic installations are only one form—pollute it to the point where it is by no means certain that it will be adequate even to the needs of his own children, not to mention those who come after them.

When one ponders these evils, one sees that they point to two deficiencies in outlook. The first is the restriction of the consciousness of obligation to the needs of the present generation alone—the self-centeredness that regards nature as an instrument and the convenience of contemporary man as an end in itself, as though there were no past and no future and as though man were not himself a part of nature. I would plead for an end to this arrogant and hopeless attitude, and for the incorporation into public philosophy of the West of the recognition of the obligation to pass this planet on to future generations in a state no poorer, no less fair, no less capable of supporting the wonder of life, than that in which we found it.

But second, I think these evils also have to do with the cult of production-for-production's sake, and with the fetish of economic growth as an absolute good, which pervades the thinking of our time. About the desirability of economic growth to the point where basic material needs can be assured for anyone who wants to work, there can be no argument. But beyond this point?

In my own country, the idea of economic growth has become such a fetish that a healthy economy is assumed to be possible only within a context of indefinite expansion.

But why? Has this been thought through? Growth means a condition of instability, a condition devoid of equilibrium, with no prospect of permanence, leading eventually, by iron logic, to one form or another of crisis. Surely, not all the values to be sought in Western life are to be found in quantitative increase. One could have more respect, in fact, for an ideology which showed man how to live successfully in a quantitatively stable context, but with real possibilities for qualitative progress, than for one which abandons itself to a process of endless expansions, the ultimate results of which are beyond calculation and control, but almost certainly undesirable.

For this reason I think that the second thing we have to do is to learn to ask ourselves the simple but shattering question "Why growth?" and to incorporate the answer into whatever view we take of the ends of industrial society.

Finally, there is the question of the effects of contemporary industrialism on man's physical and spiritual health and on his ability to find expression—to find use for his growing leisure and escape from boredom and futility—in the cultivation of beauty. Aron makes light of this, as the customary complaint—not even entirely disinterested—of conservatives and ex-Marxists. Suffice it to say that some of us, whether conservatives or ex-Marxists, do sincerely believe that we see around us abundant evidence of the wholly uncritical adoption into our lives of devices which are on balance of doubtful benefit to the human condition, just because they appear to represent a saving of labor or a speeding up of the processes of production or daily life, and on the assumption that whatever is efficient can only be good and useful. I find this assumption unwarranted, this standard highly debatable. And I would submit that no ideology of modern industrialism can be adequate which does not embrace a thorough-going skepticism about all technological innovation beyond what is necessary to satisfy basic material needs, and a readiness to take all this under the strictest sort of public control. Let science, by all means, be free. But its application to human life must be the object of man's sharpest mistrust, and of the most severe social discipline.

All of this points, admittedly, to more dirigisme, not less, in Western society. I am sorry about this. To my mind, it is unfortunate. But I see no escape from it. The question is not whether public policy is to shape the lives of individuals. The question is whether the state is to acknowledge responsibility for that shaping of the individual life which is already occurring by the processes which it tolerates or directs. We could avoid this necessity only by renouncing altogether the fruits of scientific and technical progress and by retiring to a more primitive level of technology; and this, let me emphasize, I am not advocating.

CATLIN: From the outset, Mr. Aron confronted us with a formidable problem: the meaning of industrial society. What determines this meaning—economics, material conditions, technological development, or can ideology develop independently of the technological evolution? To what degree does this evolution offer an opportunity for communities which enable man to fulfill his role as *homo faber?* These are the problems that face both East and West.

If we accept the Marxist economic-materialistic thesis, the Soviet world is conditioned and dominated by the problems of heavy industry emerging out of a peasant agriculture. It thus conforms to the general trends of industrial society in the age of coal and steel, but for the Soviets the case is considerably exaggerated. Whatever our views or assessment may be regarding the prerogatives of local government, small-scale private ownership, the respect for small individual enterprise, and the freedom of the self-employed, this individualistic democracy is badly out of tune with large concentrations of factories and assembly-line methods. It may be that the electric—or atomic— energy supplied to some Bengali village industry will correct the Victorian tendency to concentrate industry near the key resources of coal and steel, a tendency which still exists in Russia and even more so in the backward countries. Moreover, for the well-paid worker a dichotomy between the occupations and general aspect of factory hours and those of leisure hours can modify this situation. Yet it does exist, and if it goes on uncorrected such a situation will favor the "man-lost-in-the-crowd" and an oligarchical hierarchy of leadership; it is diametrically opposed to the Catholic sociological principles of the family. We may consider this situation profoundly unhealthy, but it does correspond to the efficiency required by a system where production is constantly increasing as the society evolves toward the stage of economic growth known as The Affluent Society. Although this Affluent Society, as it exists in North America, is consumer conscious and oriented toward a competitive setup, it too has its problems. Among them are the rise of advertising and commercial materialism, evils generally lacking in more primitive societies where heavy industry is king and the needs or wants of the consumer are largely ignored.

I would like to discuss these questions in a more theoretical way, from three different, and perhaps even contradictory, standpoints: political science, political philosophy, and, finally, politics.

Professor Aron bade us compare the vast technological evolution on the one hand and the development of ideology on the other. To this I would add a third factor we cannot ignore: the extraordinary "demographical explosion" which poses very grave threats to the freedom of the individual. Is it, as some people maintain, necessary for the state to determine what the optimum population is and, using the means at its disposal, set this figure as a goal? This is one of the most compelling subjects of our time, and I thought I should mention it before I begin.

First, the point of view of political science. It is my contention that, contrary to what the Marxists claim, politics is not explainable in economic terms. In fact, political phenomena are not subject to *uni causa* explanations. The best way to grasp them is to start with power. To attain any objective, it is necessary to exert the influence of power, which has its own technique and its own conditions of efficaciousness.

I would like to stress, however, that there is not only one form of power, nor do we have to conceive of it solely in terms of the power of the state. The sovereign state as we know it today is a historical phenomenon which emerged in the seventeenth century and is perhaps on its way out. Any political science which is conceived solely in terms of the laws and decrees which emanate from the state and the solicitations and requests addressed to the state is a restrictive and sterile mode of thought. Power may be thought of as "control exercised effectively," but co-operation is also power. This is no mere academic remark.

We are beginning to learn how true this is as it applies to industry. In fact, there is a new technique of industrial relations based squarely on this hypothesis. The doctrine of co-operation ought not to be considered a utopian idea vainly opposed to the realities of power, but must be used as a vital and constructive element in the analysis of power.

Thus I refrain from thinking of "liberty" and "authority" as opposites; on the contrary, they belong to the same complex, and the displacement of authority generally associated with the practice of freedom demonstrates what I like to call "the political market" which is analogous to the economic market.

Political science itself is only interested in means. It is scientific insofar as it attempts to analyze and verify the correlations between the facts and hypotheses that have been formulated. It does not concern itself with ends; there is only one end—the maintenance of civil peace.

In the field of political philosophy, we are no longer dealing with means but with ends. And here we are immediately confronted with a basic question: is it a fact that we must hunt for the *Gemeinschaft*—to borrow Tönnies' terminology—or be content with a *Gesellschaft?*

Soviet society aims at complete conformity of thought, and its whole academic system tends in this direction. In this society, allegiance to orthodoxy is a strict prerequisite for political success. How far can we in the West go in this direction? To what extent are we "weakened" by the lack of conformity—or "harmony"—in Western society? Does the notion of "political market" which we rightly cherish presuppose that we hold all opinions, of whatever kind, as "equal under law" or does it adapt itself to what some authors have named "a legitimate line of thought" which would itself be liberal?

In approaching this vital question, we should bear in mind that the *Gemeinschaft,* or community, is—as Aristotle and Rousseau have shown—the source of all good, but also the source of almost all evil. Herein lies the truly tragic problem: the *Gemeinschaft* is the source of civic pride and virtue, but it is also the Nazis parading in Munich. Finally, can we hope that "enlightened men"—and I am not referring to an aristocracy, or to an "elite"—will lead us toward a liberal rather than a barbaric form of community? I am not wholly pessimistic on this score, but it will take a great deal of courage on the part of the educators.

I suspect that a basis may be found through a revival of Natural Law. I in no way take this to mean something deduced from principles, but an empirical construction inspired by the idea of man's vocation and the practical verification of what leads to his self-fulfillment.

Personally, I am not appealing for the "natural rights" which can authentically be based on Natural Law, but can also be seasoned with the personal preferences of some eminent philosophers. There is a "right to work," but it may offer some inconveniences if, for instance, it intrudes upon the privileges of medical unions to register the candidates and choose among them. There is an undeniable right to freedom of expression and a free press, even if this press, founded on the principle of success, proves itself to be "provocative, personal and aggressive." This freedom is seldom understood to be the right of every citizen to have his views published in the "Letters to the Editor" column of the daily newspapers, especially if those views conflict with the editorial and oligarchical policy. Actually, "freedom of the press" is unjustly reserved for a few magnates of the press who are not curbed by any considerations of national responsibility, whose overriding concern is profit for themselves and their stockholders, and who feed the public—their victim—any sensational news they think will titillate it. There is, of course, a democratic right to a free press; and free discussion, in which everyone—not just those approved by the Establishment—participates, is a natural right inseparable from the development of a truly free press. But that is all. A pornographic press must be suppressed. On this score, the Soviets are right. There should be no confusion between democratic rights and commercial vulgarity. All these so-called "natural rights" are not absolute and inalienable and have to be interpreted according to the functions they fulfill. I submit that Natural Law thus understood should be the *vis directiva* of society and should in no way be confused with the *vis coactiva*.

I come finally to the plane of practical politics. One can argue that democracy tends toward hedonism, evaluates the immediate interests of all the citizens indiscriminately, refuses to admit that one aspiration is not as good as another, and is wary of the possible significance of an "educated society." We may well wonder whether an accord could even be reached in a democracy on the question of educational, moral, or philosophical values. There are those who contend that only a democracy governed by a conscious avant-garde—an aristocracy—is sufficiently competent, but there are conspicuous dangers in a society of a self-appointed elite. Here is a worth-while and ambitious project for the political scientists: too long have they repeated the cliché that democracy as we know it may not be a perfect system of government, but no one (thanks to their professional sloth) has thought of a better one. It is high time, some one should tell them, for this situation to be corrected.

On the question of the "internal political market," I admit I am inclined to think that we should formalize public opinion polls. I would greatly like to know from week to week my fellow citizens' thinking on specific questions; to my mind, this is a much more concrete democratic method than elections at four- or five-year intervals, with the voters having to make up their minds on a whole undifferentiated mass of issues. This proposal to formalize public opinion polls is radical—very radical—but is purely democratic.

I should next like to look at the *Gemeinschaft* from the practical standpoint. Here we find what I shall call the "alienation of the intellectual." We discuss things among ourselves and are mutually quite smug. But it seems to me important that the intellectual should deign to consider the motivations of the ordinary man—and I am not thinking solely of those which give birth to revolutions. The primary problem of the ordinary man is, in my opinion, his realization that he *is* ordinary. This is why he feels so alone, and he yearns for something which will give his life meaning. This is one of the fundamental weaknesses of the Western world: we are led to ignore things which are attractive on a nonintellectual level and tend to lend meaning to the lives of ordinary men. Lacking guidance, they turn to more boorish solutions, and this bespeaks the defeat of the educator: he does not entice people away from the roughest, most unpolished form to the more profound and subtle forms of the community.

As for our relations with the Soviet world, I am very hopeful that our talks with our Russian colleagues in all branches of the social sciences will be productive. When I was with them at the Congress of Sociology at Stresa, I had the feeling that what they heard about co-operation as a political technique did not fall on deaf ears.

What I most want to discuss, however, is something I deem feasible on the so-called "Atlantic" scale. Gilbert Murray used to say that the true basis of sovereignty, as well as the veritable obstacle to its abuse, was the "community of values." My feeling is that there are certain countries with basic common values which could serve as the cornerstone of common political institutions. The most important political development since the war is the European Common Market. Can we possibly build something on a broader scale? I am sure we can. The term will be the "Atlantic Community," although it is too restrictive, for I foresee India and Australia as part of it.

The geographical delimitation is unimportant. What matters is peoples exchanging the keys to their homes, so to speak. What an example this would be to the rest of the world! "The task of our time," Helmuth von Moltke has said, "is to restore the picture of humanity to the hearts of men," and I am fully confident that the system, which takes its inspiration from Natural Law, will ultimately prevail.

Let me resume my position by saying that it is based on Christian humanism and the philosophy of advisory leadership. I expect nothing good to evolve out of a so-called "scientific humanism," which, I submit, implies an intellectualist error. I insist on the controversial term "Christian" in "Christian humanism" because I believe that our political theory might tend toward a new philosophy of an "aristocratic—advisory" sort. This kind of neo-Confucian respect for scholars and artists has already appeared in the elite of the Soviet system. But I am fearful of the power of this elite unless it is offset by the specifically Christian doctrine of an authentic brotherhood, as opposed to the notion of the original sin of pride. This is basically a religious idea and is in no way related to science.

KENNAN: I am in complete agreement with nine-tenths of what Professor Catlin says. There is only one of his ideas which makes me shudder, that is, his suggestion that we should be governed by polls. This seems to me a Jeffersonian heresy, diametrically opposed to the principles of the American *Federalist* which forms the basis of my own political ideas.

But there is one principle conspicuous by its absence in this discussion. We have not paid sufficient attention to the limitations of public life or emphasized the relatively minor role of all the aspects of public life—institutions, administration, and economy—in determining the individual's well-being. At the risk of appearing lugubrious, I submit that the human condition comprises an element we might term "tragic," in that it is immutable, it does not change no matter what pressure man exerts on the surrounding environment. I am thinking of the ephemeral and abbreviated nature of human experience, the infirmities of the body, the frequent injustice of chance, the solitude and etiolation of bereavement, the endless succession of conflicts which arise between the physical and emotional instincts of man and civilization, that is, what Freud so aptly termed *Das Unbehagen in der Kultur* (The Malaise of Civilization). To my mind, these difficulties represent limitations imposed on human well-being which public authority is helpless to correct. Throughout the highly interesting discussion of Messianism, I could not help thinking of my Scotch Calvinist ancestors, who I am sure were the worst kind of Puritans imaginable and would have judged the idea of a terrestrial paradise the worst sort of blasphemy. What I want to underscore is that there were religious beliefs based on the idea than man is strictly limited in helping himself, and this considerably circumscribed the possibilities of Messianic thought.

Given these circumstances, it seems to me there is relatively little man can hope to do for himself using the various instruments we have mentioned in speaking of political and economic administration. The most he can hope for is to accede to the living conditions most propitious for physical and psychic health, integrate himself into an environment conducive to the extreme variations of the needs and capabilities of the individual. This environment should at the same time provide an outlet for man's work, his curiosity, his capacity to give himself and wax enthusiastic, a means of expression for his frequent desire to feel useful and for his basic altruism, and even for his aggressiveness and love of danger. This last is especially important as it applies to the pressing problem of juvenile delinquency. The outlets I have in mind are those which offer the opportunity of fully exploiting various facets of the human personality in a way which is not wholly inconsistent and to lead a life which is rich and varied enough to seem a reasonable compensation for its brevity and unpleasantness.

This is an increasingly acute problem, especially in my country, where leisure is already becoming an important factor because we are approaching the final stage of industrial evolution. Millions of Americans now have at least two free days a week and there is even talk of making it three (many people in fact already have three days off). The question of what they will do with this free time, or how they will be encouraged or instructed to put it to use, has been left up to laissez faire and individual choice. If you asked the average American about the adaptation, he would doubtless reply: "It's very simple. The possibilities of leading a good life are there, it's up to the individual to make up his own mind and not the government or any elite group or brain trust to decide what is best for him or what he needs." This is obvious, but the fact remains that many Americans are depressed, dissatisfied, and terrified at the idea of having this leisure time on their hands. This is why we think —or at least why I think—that this answer is insufficient. As Mr. Galbraith has emphasized in his *The Affluent Society,* there is considerable overproduction of goods which can be manu- factured and sold commercially, but an underproduction of pub- lic and social services. As far as the possibilities of a good life are concerned, services are fully as important as consumer goods. This imbalance seems more and more disturbing.

I submit that in these circumstances government policy ought not be to tell the individual where his interests lie or what the "good life" should consist of, for this would in all probability be disastrous and lead to some hideous totalitarianism. But it does seem to me that those in positions of authority in a com- munity—and by this rather vague definition I mean not only those in official positions but also anyone who might exert an influence on the possibilities of a "good life"—should try to see that the individual can make useful and favorable choices at each stage of his life and do everything in their power to make certain it is reasonably easy for him to choose good.

A few examples will illustrate my thinking. We should use every means at our disposal to make sure that this choice is open to children as well, although theirs should be a much more limited selection. I think that we Americans have to move quickly to spare our children from choosing stimulants which overexcite them, get them into trouble, and lead to the creation of such conditions as already exist in several of our large cities.

I also believe the government should be made partly responsi- ble for the educational methods of children at home. It seems to me quite abnormal that when children are charged with a crime or misdemeanor—and in my country the rate of juvenile delinquency is extremely high—they alone appear in court and are found guilty while their parents walk out scot free.

But first let us discuss the choices open to adults. Again, a few examples. Although personally I loathe the automobile and would be delighted to see it disappear from our lives as a means of transportation, I would not go so far as to outlaw it by dictatorial methods. Yet I think the state should see to it that every individual could decide whether he preferred traveling by car or train. At the rate things are going now in the United States, in a very few years our people will no longer have this choice. Along this same line of thinking, I think every person with a television set should have the right to choose whether he wants to look at trash or at programs of real artistic merit; here again I am far from certain this choice will long exist. Of course the individual can still make a choice today, but in my opinion it is a very limited one. Far be it from me to force anyone to read good books, but I think that everyone should have free and easy access to something besides works of history or current events, for instance. I shudder to think what the future would hold in store for us if we were to allow publishing to be dominated by advertising as television is today. When I think about it, I come to a conclusion which most of my colleagues will find shocking: American civilization will be healthy only when advertising will have been separated—and kept separated—from any form of real literature and all news media. This would require a revolution in the financing of the written word, but I submit that such a revolution is indispensable. The way things are going, advertising will soon control not only the magazines—which they do already—but books as well, that is, the last type of publication it does not finance.

Finally, I have no intention of forcing man to leave the cities and go commune with nature, but I would like him to have this possibility if he so desired. It is therefore incumbent on us to protect our countryside and preserve the natural beauties of our environment. This is being done in Europe, but in the United States and all countries moving toward overindustrialization and overpopulation this presents a real danger.

I would like to stress that the objective is not to prohibit by force the vulgarity and triviality of leisure and amusements, but to offer another possibility. It is a matter of preserving a minority or, if you prefer, an elite—to borrow Mr. Catlin's expression—a minority with different tastes which can in a way serve as an example of the good life. I do not really believe that this "second possibility" will be understood or adopted by very many people if there is not a distinguished nucleus of fine minds to set an example. I would like our civilization to be such that these people can continue to appear and live among us.

You may well wonder, as I do, what the chances are for a democratic state—I mean one which really chooses its representatives from among the middle classes as in the United States and not from an intellectual or artistic elite—ever to understand or apply what I am trying to say. I have to admit the chances are small and that nothing similar will happen in the near future, certainly not in my lifetime. But we must think of our children and their world, of our children's children, and so on indefinitely. For their sake, I propose that we form what I shall call a "protest minority" which would lay stress on these facets of life, devote itself to them above all, and solemnly declare that it would support only those political philosophies which pay them due heed.

HERSCH: Professor Catlin stresses that today the average man is lonely, and I believe that this is a rankling sore of our Western defense. I really think that this solitude is perhaps the point at which we are most vulnerable to totalitarian ideologies.

I would also like to say how much I appreciated what Mr. Kennan had to say about the irreducible aspect of the tragic in human existence, that which is not dependent on social organization. But I would prefer to go a little further regarding the solutions he suggested, such as the solution to the problem of leisure in the United States. I maintain that even if there is a "reasonable stake of choices," even if there are various possibilities for leisure of a more respectable sort than that presently available, the question is not resolved. I must admit that the picture of humanity utilizing its worthy leisure watching high-class shows is more than I can bear. I submit that if this leisure is to mean anything, people will have to believe in something to begin with. And they will have to believe in or care about *this* thing, not something else. In other words, over and above the choices available there has to be an inner necessity, which is more important than the choice. And when you believe in something, you are vulnerable; you must be prepared to suffer for whatever you cherish. I have just spent six months in the United States, and I have the impression that what is most lacking in America is the willingness to believe deeply enough in something to suffer for it.

SPERBER: To comment on both Mr. Kennan's and Miss Hersch's remarks, I suspect that the problem of solitude in society and the other problems posed by mass culture, such as the improper use of leisure time, do exist because we find ourselves faced with possibilities never before known. After all, the fairs that came to town once or twice a year were no better than most of the television or radio fare we're offered, and God knows I find that bad, even insulting. So we do have a new problem but it is a "newness" which denotes the emergence of a new sensitivity. The flight from boredom is as old as mankind, as old as history. What *is* new is the fact that now the most important industry seems to be the satisfaction of this world bored with itself. When Miss Hersch talks about solitude and through a misunderstanding can imply that solitude is more real, more sensitive on this side of the Iron Curtain than the other (I know that is not what she meant), I should like to clarify this by saying that man's solitude, like mortality, is his incurable illness. The question is to ascertain the degrees of solitude through which man can pass and whether the experience leads downward toward a deforming baseness or upward toward an acute awareness and new sensations and perceptions (what is called, from a Greek word rife with meaning, "aesthetics"). I submit that the industrial civilization, in spite of all reproaches made to it, is making it possible for the aesthetic world to grow and spread.

ROSTOW: I shall try to respond to the questions which conclude Mr. Aron's written statement, not with an answer, but with another question, more rhetorical than interrogatory—"Are we so badly off?"

Here I think Montesquieu can provide a useful perspective. You will recall that Montesquieu stressed two great themes. First, he pointed out that each culture is unique, and that the goals, values, and forms of a legal system had to be a function of the uniqueness of the culture which produced them. But with equal emphasis, he had his own views about systems of law and about the spirit of law which animated them. He expressed definite and categorical value judgments about which systems were in his view better than others. His scheme of preferences is the incarnation of "the natural law of progress" so characteristic of the eighteenth century. For him the republican form of government was the ultimate goal and objective of social life.

Considered in relation to Montesquieu's analysis, Mr. Aron's question becomes that of determining the extent to which a "natural law" or common philosophy as to the goals of social organization could now be generally accepted—or, in somewhat different terms, to decide whether the countries of the East and of the West, those of Asia, Europe, Africa, and North and South America, despite their diversity, share a core of values which in fact determines the lines of their development, and for which they are ready to fight. In this connection, I believe we all recognize the wisdom of Mr. Asoka Mehta's thesis, that the diversity of political means employed by different societies conceals a profound unanimity of goals. The myth, or the image of the ideal which people have as to the desirable way of organizing society, is to a large extent accepted by everybody. I don't mean to imply that people everywhere would agree as to the details of organizing courts and parliaments. But one can nonetheless speculate as to whether the values men seek in social organization do not have a common content throughout the world: equal opportunity, equality in prestige and in respect, a certain measure of economic progress, of progress in justice and in social well-being, certain shared views as to the organization of power, and the protection of the individual against the omnipotence of the state.

Many speak of apathy among the young, of their lack of fervor, and the absence of a Messianic conviction behind our faith in liberty. This complaint is as old as the world. It may be that this apathy does in fact prevail, although it does not correspond to the views I have formed about the young people who come each year to attend classes at Yale, with their skepticism, their energy, their passion, and their idealism. I am convinced that if modern techniques for measuring opinion had been applied to the youth of Hungary a month before the revolution in 1956, the polls would have shown that they were conformist, disillusioned, and apathetic. In fact, as the event proved, they were far from possessed by such sentiments. I hesitate to conclude that the religion of liberty is no longer a fighting faith, and that Milton, Locke, Voltaire, Montesquieu, John Stuart Mill, and Oliver Wendell Holmes have lost their power to stir the loyalty of the young.

Modern politics are rather boring. A review of the goals of politics indicates that a large part of the population is absorbed by other problems, perhaps more important and more constructive. Given this state of things, is it wrong to affirm that the essential purpose of social organization is to protect individual liberty for its own sake, and that we love liberty not for what it does, not as a means to assure economic productivity, but as a good in itself, an end, the highest goal we can imagine for social organization, after many centuries of experience?

To define and protect the scope of individual liberty within a functioning society, the United States as you know possesses an institution of judicial control which is peculiar to its political system. The workings of our system of judicial review frequently require the Supreme Court of the United States to decide, and to discuss before the entire country, vital and fundamental cases in which liberty conflicts with order. I could cite fifty or sixty cases of this character, which arose during the last few years. Cases of this order keep alive, among the leading preoccupations of the American people, and of all concerned with the law, the endless debate about the basic meaning of social liberty, and the fundamental problems of accommodating liberty and order.

This is the reason, I suggest, why the boring quality of Western politics need not unduly worry us. The heavy burden which individual liberty imposes on man, the responsibility for making decisions he must accept because he is free, the opportunity for self-expression which Western liberty offers him, within a protected social order: these are the essential problems modern man confronts. And they are reasons, too, which permit us to hope for his progress as a human being whose first aim is life itself, who seeks solutions for his loneliness and responsibility, and who asks of society its protection, in order to be free to love, to understand, and to live.

SECTION B—SPECIALIZATION AND COMMON DISCOURSE

OPPENHEIMER: In these remarks I shall address myself to one of the questions raised in Aron's paper:

If, outside the sphere of science, there is nothing but arbitrary decision, has the result of the progress of science and scientific reasoning merely been to place in the keeping of unreason the thing that concerns us most, that is to say, the definition and choice of the essential, of the good life, of the good society?

What I have to say is really intended as an introduction. On the one hand, the problems of political philosophy are, for all the general human weight of this branch of study, highly technical in themselves and I must leave to the many here who are experts the expert discussion of this field.

On the other hand, I will perhaps talk a little more broadly, because my concern is not only with how we can hope to see a revival of political philosophy, but with a rather larger question: how can we hope to see a revival of all philosophy? In his question Aron speaks of "the choice of the essential"; that is, after all, what a cultivated skeptic says when he means metaphysics; the choice of "the good life," which is what the cultivated skeptic means when he thinks ethics; and "the good society," which is then the subject of political philosophy. I also must admit that nothing that I see in terms of action can in this area have immediate effects. I have the impression that we are here dealing with deep and only partially understood and only partially manageable human attitudes.

The question with which I am going to concern myself is the relations between the scientific explosions of this age and the weight and the excellence that we may hope to achieve in common discourse.

I have in mind an image of common discourse, which is itself blurred by three related realities. One is the size of our world and its communities, the number of people involved. One is the generally egalitarian and inclusive view in which there are no a priori restrictions on who is to participate in the discourse; clearly, not everyone will; but I think it is the essence of the Western hope that everyone may. The third is the extraordinary rapidity with which the preoccupations and circumstances of our life are altered.

What I am concerned with is an ideal, an image of a part of human life which is inherently not all-inclusive, but which has a quality of being public—I do not mean governmental, I mean universal—which speaks in terms intelligible to all, of things accessible to all, of meanings relevant to all. I would not, for instance, say that the microbiologists belong to this public sector. I would not regard the modern painter as part of the public sector, and certainly not those advanced and experimental elements of the art of musical composition, where, I have been led to believe, these men, as in the pure mathematician's art, are concerned with the very high purpose of preserving the vigor and integrity and life of their own skills, but are not, in the first instance, addressing themselves to man at large.

This image of the public sector has also suffered from the growth of science itself. I would like to make a few comments on the nature of the relations between rational discourse, culminating in philosophical discourse, on the one hand, and the development of science, on the other hand.

I am very much guided by my own limited experience in the United States; and when I talk, I will think of our universities, of our symposia such as this one, of our mass culture, of the ways in which Americans use their leisure, of what is thought, and written, and done in the country I know best.

For this provincialism, I make only the following two excuses: it is what I know at first hand; I am very distrustful of the traveler's impressions of other countries. But more important, it seems to me that in the United States we are perhaps the first to arrive at an era in which production for consumption's sake has reached a kind of completeness; I am aware that it is not fully complete, but it is, from the point of view of men at large, largely complete. We are also among the first to face the problem of what to do with the leisure and the life so returned. What is it for, how does one spend it? I know that in Europe, where egalitarianism is less strong, where the intellectual tradition and the need for order are more strong, these problems are slightly less advanced and less acute than in our country. I expect, though I would gladly be told that I was wrong by historians or prophets, that the American troubles are forerunners of troubles which will not long remain out of Europe. I do not believe these troubles are as acute in communist countries, even in Russia. The technological revolution is not as far along; the land of plenty is not as near; and, in addition, the unifying presence of tyranny has greatly affected, not the nature of intellectual activity in those domains where it is free, but the contours of the regions where intellectual activity as such can be free. Therefore, I believe that in studying the American scene, we may be reminded, not how to do things, not what to do all over the world in the same way, but of some of the dangers which accompany the fulfillment of the basic premises of the industrial and technological revolution, and some of the hopes.

I hardly need bring to mind that the great sciences of today arose in philosophical discourse and in technical invention. All of natural science has its origins in an undifferentiated, unspecialized common human discourse. The question is, therefore, why the enormous success, the unanticipated, not fully appreciated, and at the moment not fully realized—I would say never to be fully realized—success of one sort of intellectual activity should not have had a beneficial effect on the intellectual life of man. In some ways it has, because certain forms of extreme superstition, certain insistent ways of provincialism have found themselves unable to flourish in the presence of the new light of scientific discovery.

But if we think back to the early days, either of the European tradition or of modern society, we see that we were there dealing with relatively few people. The citizenry of Athens, the few handfuls of men who concerned themselves with the structure of American political power, the participants in the eighteenth-century Enlightenment were relatively few in number. They had before them a relatively well-digested and common language, experience, and tradition, and a common basis of knowledge. It is true that already in the eighteenth century, physics, astronomy, and mathematics were beginning to assume these specialized and abstract and unfamiliar aspects which have increasingly characterized these subjects up to the present day. But they were not beyond the reach of laymen. They were perhaps greeted by laymen with an enthusiasm which a fuller knowledge would not have supported, but they were part of the converse of the eighteenth century.

If we look today, we see a very different situation, an alienation between the world of science and the world of public discourse, which has emasculated, impoverished, intimidated the world of public discourse without any countervailing advantage, except to the specialized sciences, and which in a strange sense, to use a word which political scientists have taught me, has denied to public discourse an element of legitimacy, has given it a kind of arbitrary, unrooted, unfounded quality. Thus any man may say what he thinks, but there is no way of arriving at a clarification or a consensus.

In the past, common discourse and its queen, philosophy, rested on an essentially common basis of knowledge; that is, the men who participated knew, by and large, the same things and could talk of them with a reasonable limitation in the ambiguity of what they were saying. There was a relatively stable, and a deeply shared, tradition, a historic experience which was common among the participants in the conversation, and a recognition—not always explicit and often, in fact, denied—of a difference between the kind of use and value which public discourse has as its high ideal, and the kind of criteria by which the sciences themselves in part must judge themselves. I want to say here that the traits which are important in public discourse are enormously important in science; and a lack of recognition of this has created great blocks, great repugnancies on the part of humane, cultivated, and earnest men in their appreciation of the natural sciences and of even the abstract sciences.

I speak of a recognition that there are things important to discuss and analyze, to explore, to subject to some logical surgery, to have in order, things which are not best viewed as propositional truth, which are not assertions, verifiable by the characteristic methods of science, as to the existence in the world of this or that connection between one thing and another.

They have rather a normative and thematic quality. Such, indeed, is the intention of this discussion. They assert the connectedness of things, the relatedness of things, the priority of things; and without them there would be no science; without them there could be no order in human life. But they do not say that the value of a certain constant—measuring the elementary electric charge in rational units—is 137.037, and challenge you to see what is the next decimal point. They permit no analogous verification. I do not insist that the poet speaks the truth; he speaks something equally important. He may, but very seldom, speak the truth: he speaks meanings, and he speaks order.

Thematic, as opposed to propositional, discourse is the typical function of the public sector of our lives, from where law, morality, and the highest forms of art arise. It is not best construed, though it can occasionally be construed, as assertions of fact about the natural order or the human order. It is best construed as assertions of experience, of dedication, of commitment. We all know how great is the gulf between the intellectual world of the scientist and the intellectual world, hardly existing today, of public discourse on fundamental human problems.

One of the reasons is that the scientific life of man which, in my opinion, constitutes an unparalleled example of our power and our virtuosity and our dedication, has grown both quantitatively and qualitatively in ways which, to Pythagoras and Plato, would have seemed very, very strange, and even nefarious, and which cast a shadow over Newton's later years, as he saw what might come. Purcell, who is a professor of physics at Harvard, said a year or two ago: "Ninety per cent of all scientists are alive." A friend of ours, a historian much concerned with Hellenistic and sixteenth- and seventeenth-century science, did himself a small exercise—to plot, as a function of time, the number of people engaged in the acquisition of new knowledge, which is a definition of science. It is, for about the past 200 years, an exponential function of the time, and the characteristic period is ten years. A similar plot of the publications in science follows the same law.

Now you may say, you will want to say, you will argue with me, that none of this is serious—that there are a few great discoveries, a few great principles that anyone can master and understand, and that all these details are really not of any great importance in human life.

Of course, many of the details are not; they are not even of importance in the life of the sciences. We make mistakes, but, by and large, the volume of publication is a rather accurate professional judgment of what needs to be known in order to get on. And I ask you to believe that in this growth there are insights, there are spectacles of order and harmony, of subtlety, of wonder, which are comparable to the great discoveries which we learned in school. I ask you also to believe that they are not easily communicated in terms of today's ordinary experience and tongue. They rest on traditions, some of which are very old, involving experience and language that has been cherished, refined, corrected, sometimes for centuries, sometimes for decades. And that is one reason why, if you were to ask me what the foundations of science are, what is the point, what is this all about, I could not answer. This is partly because sciences are ramified; they deal with different kinds of harmony. And none of them can be completely reduced to others. They are in themselves a plural and multiple reflection of reality.

But it is partly also that the principles which are general, which, from the logical point of view, imply a great deal about the natural order of the world, have had to be couched in terms which themselves have had a long human history of definition, refinement, and subtilization. If you were to ask me what is the great law of the behavior of atoms, not as we now talk about them, but as they were talked about in the early years of this century, I could certainly write it on the blackboard and it would not occupy much space; but to give some sense of what it is all about would be for me a very great chore, and for you a very earnest and unfamiliar experience.

The specialization of science is also a thing which is hard to appreciate outside the practitioners. We do not, in the fields of science, know each other very well. There are many crosslinkages. There are, as far as I know, no threats of contradiction. There is a pervasive relevance of everything to everything else. There are analogies, largely formal, mathematical analogies, which stretch as far as from things like language to things like heat engines. But there is no logical priority of one science over another. There is no deduction of the facts of living matter from the facts of physics. There is simply an absence of contradiction. And the criteria of order, of harmony, of generality, and of coherence, which are as much a part of science as the rectitude of observations and the correctness of logical manipulation— these criteria are *sui generis* from science to science.

In addition to this, the sense of openness, to some extent of accident, of incompleteness, of infinity, which the study of nature brings, is of course very discouraging to public discourse, because it is impossible to get it all and whole; it is impossible to master it; it is impossible to summarize it; it is impossible to close it off. It is a growing thing, the ends of which are probably coextensive with the ends of civilized human life.

This is a set of circumstances which has largely deprived our public discourse of its first requirement: a common basis of knowledge. I will not say what bad effects it may have had on philosophical discourse—that a whole category of human achievement which grew from philosophy and invention is shut off from the thoughts of the philosophers and of ordinary men. I will not say with certainty whether, in excluding this kind of order and this kind of verifiability, one has not impoverished the discourse; I believe that one has. But in any case, it is a hard thing, as I know from other examples, to talk about our situation, and to have to say "I leave out, I leave aside, I leave as irrelevant, something which is as large, as central, as humane, and as moving a part of the human intellectual history as the development of the sciences themselves."

I believe that this is not an easy problem. I believe that it is not possible to have everyone well informed about what goes on, to have a completely common basis of knowledge. We do not have it ourselves in the sciences—far from it. I have the most agonizing troubles, and I would say on the whole, fail, when I try to know what the contemporary mathematicians are doing and why. I learn with wonder, but as an outsider and an amateur, what the biochemists and the biophysicists are up to. But I have one advantage; that is, there is a small part of one subject that I know well enough to have deep in me the sense of knowledge and of ignorance. And this is not perhaps wholly unattainable on a much wider scale. It is perhaps not wholly out of the question to restore to all of us a good conscience about our reason, by virtue of the fact that we are in touch with some of its most difficult and some of its most brilliant, and some of its most lovely operations.

As to the question of a stable, shared tradition, I have of course been talking about philosophy in a predominantly secular culture. I have not included as part of the sources of tradition a living revelation, or a living ecclesiastical authority. It is not so much that I wish to exclude it; but if our deliberations are to have general contemporary meaning, they must take into account the fact that our culture is secular, and may well have to develop as a secular culture. Our tradition, strong though it is—and I think the European tradition may vie with the Chinese and the Indian in this respect—is buffeted by the eruption of change. You are all aware of how unprepared we were for the tragedies of the twentieth century when it opened, and how bitter, corrosive, and indigestible many of them have been. I think primarily of the two World Wars and the totalitarian revolutions. But take one example. We certainly live in the heritage of a Christian tradition. Many of us are believers; but none of us is immune from the injunctions, the hopes, and the order of Christianity. I find myself profoundly in anguish over the fact that no ethical discourse of any nobility or weight has been addressed to the problem of the new weapons, of the atomic weapons. There has been much discussion of the problems of security, of strategy, of the balance of powers. This is recent, and I welcome it, because as little as five or six years ago, there was no discussion of any kind; that was certainly worse. But what are we to make of a civilization which has always regarded ethics as an essential part of human life, and which has always had in it an articulate, deep, fervent conviction, never perhaps held by the majority, but never absent; a dedication to "ahimsa," the Sanskrit word that means "doing no harm or hurt," which you find in the teachings of Jesus and Socrates—what are we to think of such a civilization, which has not been able to talk about the prospect of killing almost everybody, except in prudential and game-theoretic terms?

Of course, people *do*. Thus Lord Russell writes, as do others: "But these people want heaven and earth too. They are not in any way talking about deep ethical dilemmas, because they deny that there are such dilemmas. They say that if we behave in a nice way, we will never get into any trouble." But that, surely, is not ethics.

In 1945, in 1949, perhaps now, there have been crucial moments in which the existence of a public philosophical discourse, not aimed at the kind of proof which the mathematicians give, not aimed at the kind of verifiability which the biologists have, but aimed at the understanding of the meaning, of the intent, and of the commitment of men, and at their reconciliation and analysis, could have made a great difference in the moral climate, and the human scope of our times.

I would only like to say that in all those instances in which the West, notably my own country, has expressed the view that there was no harm in using the superweapons, provided only that they were used against an antagonist who had done some wrong, we have been in error; and that our lack of scruple, which grew historically out of the strategic campaigns of World War II, the total character of that war, and the numbing and indifference of which responsible people then complained, of which Mr. Stimson complained bitterly, has been a very great disservice to the cause of freedom and to the cause of free men.

And as to the third of the conditions of public discourse and of philosophy, this, I think, is the emphasis placed on the role of certitude, an emphasis characteristic of the Renaissance, and natural after Scholasticism. If we think of most of Plato, all the early Plato, we can hardly imagine a more useful exploration of the central ideas of high Athenian culture. Plato does not end his discussions with any summary; in that respect, they may be a model for ours. And the purpose is not the attainment of certainty. The purpose is the exploration of meaning. The purpose is the exploration of what men wish, intend, hope, cherish, love, and are prepared to do. My belief is that, if the common discourse can be enriched by a more tolerant and humane welcome for the growth of science, its knowledge, its intellectual virtue—I am not now speaking of machinery, for this is another problem—it may be more easily possible to accept the role of clarification and of commitment which is the true purpose of philosophy, and not to hang around its neck that dread, dead bird, "How can you be sure?" which has, I believe, stunted philosophy, even in its great days, its great modern days, and which has driven it actually almost out of existence at the present moment.

I would think that we could look to a future in which, very high on the list of the purposes of consumption and leisure, were knowledge and thought, a future in which the intellectual vigor of man had a greater scope than at any time in history, and in which, to quote what Mr. Rostow said, man is free to love, to live, and to know. I believe that it is largely, of course not wholly, through living, which is so deeply the function of the arts, and through knowing, which is largely the function of the sciences, that the function of the philosopher, which is loving, can be most richly supported. It is, I think, no accident that the optimistic view of the present, and especially of the American present, came from Rostow. For if you examine the situation of the Common Law, and I think, above all, of the American Common Law, you see that the common basis of knowledge, the stable shared tradition, and the recognition of the importance of non-propositional knowledge, are all highly characteristic of this community—one of the most successful communities in our century. One cannot extend that community, one cannot transplant that community to the wider framework of talking about everything; but one can learn something from its existence.

I know that, technically, the questions I have raised are formidable in a most discouraging way: How are we to learn a little more of what goes on in this world, and to be satisfied with understanding, in places where certitude is unattainable? I think we may regard the exploration of these questions as quite beyond the scope of our discussions here. But I am deeply sure of one thing, and that is that they require effort and discipline and dedication, and that, in the measure in which we come to understand the reasons for this, we may also find ways of doing it. I find it hard to believe that with the greatest intellectual activity of all time taking place in the next room, catholic, public, common understanding will be possible unless we open the doors.

ARON: Apropos of the absence of any discussion about the weapons of massive destruction, I heard Miss Hersch murmur "Karl Jaspers." Jaspers did in fact write on the subject, first a pamphlet of twenty-five pages, then a six-hundred page book that became a best seller in Germany, which proves that the subject is surely an integral part of the public discourse within the West itself and with the Soviet world.

You showed that you are perfectly well aware of the limits of this discourse by two observations you made, one at the beginning of your paper, the other at the end. The first is the realization that whenever total war means suicide for both sides, war becomes absurd, impossible, which is a remark of prudence. A Hegelian might be led to believe by such a remark that reason is still operating by guile, since it is reason which, without morally transforming man, urges him not to wage war because war has become irrational. The second observation, at once complementary and contradictory, is that man is not content with the idea of rejecting war simply because it is irrational. These two propositions can be thus combined: reason is clever enough to keep vicious men from waging war, but how preferable it would be for men to realize the folly of war itself and that exterminating man with atomic bombs is no solution to any problem. But perhaps these two complementary and contradictory propositions also show, from another standpoint, the fundamental difficulty which you underscored: how to combine the ethical and philosophical discourse which over the centuries has been the essential discourse by which men have lived, with the considerations of pragmatism and prudence which evolve either from science or from industrial society itself.

I believe that, in a most remarkable, telling, and profound way, you have made us realize that it is quite impossible to eliminate scientific knowledge from our philosophical discourse. You have also showed us that it is practically impossible to integrate the entire complex of scientific knowledge into the philosophical discourse. I suspect that the conclusion toward which you were heading was that the exact comprehension of scientific knowledge would reveal the presence—in the universe of the scholars themselves—of the essential ingredients of order and harmony out of which philosophical discourse emerges. Thus it seems to me you have simultaneously suggested the opposition but also the reconciliation. On a higher level, your paper perhaps took a more optimistic view in the middle than it did at the end, for if the constituent elements of public discourse really do lie in scientific knowledge, the last word is not the contradiction but probably something akin to reconciliation.

HERSCH: I suspect that the importance of common discourse has perhaps not diminished as much as you say, and that in past eras we may have overrated it. In painting and music, for example, we believed a common language did exist, whereas what was speaking was not really the painting or not really the music, but something in these paintings which was of another order. In this sense, contemporary artists are actually purists who are trying to eliminate the illusion of certain factors in their art. I think the same holds true for philosophy, and that the common discourse of philosophy, for example, has been more ambiguous, its common character *is* more ambiguous today than it seems to have been in antiquity, even with such lucid philosophers as Plato.

NABAKOV: I agree with Mr. Oppenheimer that the role of the arts in public discourse has, if not disappeared, at least diminished. They have, so to speak, dissociated themselves from this public discourse. I would even go further and add that I cannot actually imagine how the completely independent sector of the arts can be restored to its place in public discourse, which is so involved with social and economic problems, nor can I envisage how it can overcome its dissociation from science, with which it was so closely allied in the past. Think of a city like Venice, where for a century the applied sciences—whether in painting, drawing, or architecture—were so closely bound up with the desire to participate in the life of man, to reach mutual understanding and form a harmonious society. Today we are a far cry from such a world. And the reasons for this estrangement seem obvious to me. We are all aware that in the nineteenth century the artists—for reasons that may or may not be valid—suddenly realized they had something more to do than art. They took upon themselves new missions, new ways of perceiving and expressing themselves, and developed new techniques; in doing so they increased their power and strength, but lost the essence of what they were.

This is why today's avant-garde composer prefers the way of asceticism and returns to the internal problems of his art—the art of sound. He seeks to reform his art by grappling with the laws of sound and thus approximating something he deems comparable to science. I would rather compare it to the technique of chess. Yet this is the only way that art—or at least the art of music—can validly reintegrate itself into the "public discourse" and have a feeling of participation and responsibility.

In painting, this experiment is already under way. The most interesting example is that of Poland. I have been most impressed by the didactic presentation the Poles lend the shows they send to the Soviet Union, by their attempts to explain what their paintings mean to the general public and how they are related to the other branches of human knowledge such as poetry, philosophy, and literature. Within the modest limits of our means, our organization has tried to emulate the Polish example and recently sent a small show from Paris to Vienna. The catalogue made an attempt to explain the relationships between the graphic arts, literature, and philosophy. The public responded immediately and showed an amazing respect. This leads me to believe that the arts are trying to move in the direction of "public discourse," but I suspect they will become a part of it only after they have accomplished the difficult and sometimes painful experience of rediscovering their own nature and essence.

POLANYI: Mr. Oppenheimer expressed profound regret that the major political and military decisions of our time are made without any general discussion about the ethical problems they raise. But our cruelty and disdain of any moral consideration during the last war may be due precisely to the fact that this war saw an unprecedented wave of moral passions which manifested themselves in this violent manner. Moreover, our moral discourse is paralyzed in its own terms, so much so that any statesman who would defer to, or show any sincere interest in, moral considerations as they apply to public action would either be dismissed as a hypocrite or reduced to silence by the doubts his words would engender.

OPPENHEIMER: Perhaps I did not express myself clearly: I do not maintain that a government must be influenced by ethical discussions. I believe that it is difficult to know how much governments are capable of expressing a "consensus" or an ethical point of view; this is an extremely difficult problem to solve. What concerns me is that, in spite of Jaspers, so many days have passed and so little has been said that is worth listening to. We can ignore ethics; but it has to be there to be ignored. There is no need for man to act virtuously, but it is necessary that we discuss virtue.

POSTAN: I submit that the efficaciousness and power of ethical elements in our civilization are—for good or bad—greater today than they were in the past. I believe they are constantly increasing, even in the field of arms. Compare the lack of any moral indignation at the time TNT was invented—Nobel was a notable exception—with the effects the invention of the bomb had upon the consciences both of its inventors and those who had a hand in its development.

In democratic countries—especially during World War II— we can observe the importance of purely ethical and moral feelings by the way in which various major political or strategic decisions, including the declaration of war itself, had to be adjusted so that statesmen could forecast what public reaction would be on the ethical plane. You remember, for example, the important role played in both wars by what was termed the "propaganda of atrocities." What we tend to forget is that this "propaganda of atrocities" is a tribute paid by the state to the strength and frequency of the ethical point of view. I submit that the trouble with our democratic society is not that moral or ethical stimulants are not widespread enough, but rather that it is easier to provoke them than get rid of them. And once they have been mobilized, not only are they a major force toward converting amoral intention into a public act, they may also serve as the justification for a whole range of cruel and destructive acts, to which our era seems especially prone. The problem is not to assess the depth or breadth of the ethical content in our civilization, but to study it from the institutional and sociological standpoint and define the methods not only of mobilizing it, but especially of demobilizing it.

VOEGELIN: The question of the use of arms was discussed long before the appearance of the atomic bomb—during the 1930's, for instance, when it was a question of gas or bacteriological warfare. In fact, this is a classic question of politics, which is a part of the concept of the *bellum justum,* the "just war." One of the principal assumptions is that a war can begin as a "just war," become extremely unjust by the way it is fought, and even more unjust by the type of peaceful settlement imposed after it is over. These are questions of the most elementary sort, and I do not believe anyone should complain if we refrain from constantly bringing them up in public.

The question you pose is, I believe, essentially a sociological one. It concerns this type of society in which we live and in which an elementary knowledge perfectly acquired for centuries is not publicly efficacious. But there is a reason it is not: as you have quite rightly pointed out, an atomic bombardment is not a moral matter but depends on politics and questions of existence. And when a social process is involved, we cannot, in the name of morality, refuse to use certain types of weapons and make certain kinds of decisions. The classic treatise on this point is Thucydides' *Peloponnesian War.* The necessity of the process he terms *kinesis,* and he considers *kinesis* a kind of social illness. When you are caught in such an illness you cannot extricate yourself as long as you are a statesman; you can only get out of it personally. The Platonic attitude of withdrawal from "sick politics," in the Thucydidean sense of the term, is a personal possibility, but it does not eliminate the public necessity of taking on the sickness as long as it lasts.

OPPENHEIMER: I agree with Professor Voegelin that tradition is, of course, indispensable in dealing with any problem whatsoever. But it is equally essential that we realize when the same words are being used to describe different phenomena. I do not claim that the problem raised by the atomic bomb is new in the sense that it is unrelated to what men have done and experienced in the past. But the idea that this was resolved, whereas the subject we are concerned with was completely different, does not strike me as particularly helpful. Nor does it seem to me to correspond to what we think aside from our studies.

ARON: No, but I think that those who raise objections do not for a minute deny that *pragmatically* the extent of possible destruction does pose new problems for mankind. What we must try to determine is whether, *morally,* the problem is new. Jaspers maintains that it is, because at worst these weapons of massive destruction imply a danger of destroying humanity itself. Jaspers goes on to say—and I believe he is right—that such a situation is not a mere resurgence of the classical historical problem which we observe whenever a new weapon is developed: we had a new situation when weapons were thrown or hurled rather than used to strike directly; the same thing was true with the innovation of striking from a distance without being seen, and again when it became possible to attack a large number instead of a small. But all these innovations were part of the same whole. What Jaspers claims—and I agree—is that the "whole" is new when the arms imply a danger of destroying all mankind.

OPPENHEIMER: I agree, but I also have an answer which bears on a fundamental point: I am absolutely opposed to the idea that ethics is not a practical matter. If it is not, then it is nothing.

IYER: I contend that the reason the atomic bomb has raised a question which, while it may not be new in principle, has nevertheless introduced a new dimension, is this: as long as we focus our attention on the question of the sacredness of life, as it applies to a specific individual, it is always possible to conjure up utilitarian or discretionary arguments to justify the loss of this life in order to gain another. But now that we are threatened with the complete destruction of mankind, we find ourselves paradoxically faced with the old question: do we believe in the holiness of the life of a single person? Because we cannot elude the problem of total destruction by utilitarian reasons or reasons of prudence.

LINDBLOM: What Mr. Oppenheimer has said is basically the expression of a yearning which leaves unanswered the question of applying the program he outlined. The best way of dealing with ethical questions is not to consider them in terms which are too abstract or theoretical, but to apply them to practical, personal, or social problems.

As for the bomb—and this may be a sad commentary vis-à-vis ethics but still is fortunate for the world as a whole—the fact is that we still lack sufficient experience in the launching of bombs to formulate a set of common experiences which might serve as the basis for a new series of ethical propositions about the bomb—propositions which would transcend the plane of prudence.

On the other hand, ethics consists more of a set of attitudes which cannot be formulated than a set of standards or themes which threaten to be too rigid or to lead to narrowness or intolerance. The yearning for unity must be twice tempered. We need first of all specialized ethics for the specialized roles man plays in life; the businessman's ethics, the political leaders' ethics cannot coincide with traditional Christian morality. Then too, one of the sources of strength and stability in a democratic society is the fact that its members find a way of adjusting their conduct harmoniously without being compelled to justify it with identical reasons. We might even go so far as to say that ethics is too personal a matter for public discussion and that in a peaceful society the citizens would agree as to the circumstances under which the bomb would or would not be set off, but the reasons for this decision would remain hidden within the soul of each individual. Finally, ethics which transcends the level of prudence can develop by using the motives of prudence as a starting point.

In general, we should give closer consideration to social relations and mechanisms than did Mr. Oppenheimer.

JOUVENEL: I am quite surprised by the language used by my friend Professor Lindblom, who seems to contrast ethics based on prudence with those which have nothing to do with it. I do not know what prudence is if not the application of ethics to the actual circumstances. This is the definition of prudence. And

I am afraid that if we imagine that there are ethics which have nothing to do with prudence, we will next suppose that we can choose the ethics we need or want. Then, when we realize that these arbitrary ethics are inapplicable, we will conclude that the universe is absurd. I submit that it is absolutely essential for us to conceive of prudence as the link between our beliefs and our acts.

ARON: The word "prudence"—at least in our philosophical tradition—has two completely different meanings. There is the "prudence" of the Greek philosophers, which was the application of wisdom to specific concrete situations. By this definition you are absolutely right. But there is another meaning of the term, which assimilates it roughly to pragmatic and utilitarian considerations, and in this case you are wrong.

SECTION C—IDEOLOGIES AND PHILOSOPHY

JOUVENEL: First Professor Catlin and then Mr. Kennan have posed the problem of the "good life," a subject which in the words of Mr. Asoka Mehta constitutes the best common ground for men "from different planets." If, as I suspect, the "good life" is the *terminus ad quem* of our seminar, it follows that we should take the "good life" as the *terminus a quo* of our judgments in the social sciences. Whence certain changes I deem most desirable.

Take, for example, the science of economics. Swayed by concepts such as productivity and methods such as "econometry," we tend increasingly to consider man as a "factor of production" who has to be used as rationally as possible to effect maximum production of durable goods or objects. No doubt these goods are destined for man; but what a difference between our meticulous concern for the maximum flow of goods through the optimal utilization of man, and our neglect in researching the best use of products to achieve the optimal form of human existence!

Is it even conceivable to try and find this optimal form for "man-the-consumer" as opposed to "man-the-producer"? How can he ever know the "good life" if his existence is divided into joyless working hours and meaningless consumption hours? It would seem to me that the "good life" should presuppose that man find self-realization and self-fulfillment both in his work and in his leisure.

The idea of the "good life" can in itself furnish us a criterion for the various blessings, which differ in kind and immediate objective. For example, the national input of working hours can be equally cut by shortening the work week or by prolonging the period of schooling. It is obvious that both these diminutions, quantitatively equal, are in no wise identical from the standpoint of the "good life."

Sociology should also modify its approach. From the point of view of the good life lived by the individual—and who else can do it?—sociology is not the study of society but rather of the individual in society. Here you have such and such an individual: around him, a social context already informed and organized by others. In this environment he has to adapt himself and find self-fulfillment, and depending on whether he fails or succeeds, he either feels oppressed or discovers a possibility of expression. I think that the contrast between "oppression" and "expression" is both suitable and rife with meaning. Here then is the real sociological problem: how to insure that man— every human being—can gain access to an environment wherein he can earn the esteem and affection of his peers through self-expression and self-fulfillment.

Finally, of course, we should arrive at a radical reversal in political science. There exists a political science wrongly based on the premise that the only *potentia* is that which derives from *potestas,* from the accrual of power. But this is untrue. Such an affirmation is simply controverted by the facts and implies an unbounded optimism. On the contrary, we know that *potentia,* as Shakespeare has so wonderfully described it, takes root here and there. The problem is not that there should not be any other *potentia* except that which derives from *potestas,* but rather that all *potentia* should be considered and utilized as a *potestas.*

Let me interrupt this rapid survey of the various social sciences to pose the problem in its most general form. It is strange that for several generations the West has been able to live without the image of the "good life," without any general concept from which to judge what is best or most suited to man. Yet Descartes said that reason is the faculty which enables man to evaluate the various opportunities which are more or less within our reach and thus to apportion our efforts according to the various merits of these opportunities. In this sense, reason could be exercised only if there were a clear assumption of what man aspires to and what the "good life" consists of. And if there is no such basic premise, the classification of opportunities and the division of efforts can rely only on the irrational preferences of the moment. We may say that one of the characteristics of modern civilization is its high degree of rationality, if we consider that we in fact approach all problems rationally; but these problems are posed from unreasoned preferences which are admitted as final criteria.

In all the social sciences we flatter ourselves that we have eliminated all value judgments, but this is not, nor cannot, be true. Any comparison of objects which differ in nature presupposes the utilization of parameters. The indifference to value judgments manifests itself practically only by the utilization as *ex ante* elements of the value judgments which the conduct of men enables us to observe *ex post.* But we cannot expect that the "immediate preferences" thus noted will be either constant or coherent, as Arrow has pointed out. The rule of revealed preferences is utilitarianism, which lacks the dimension of time. As Peter Wiles has noted, we can sense it so well that in the most liberal economies the nation is compelled to save in various ways much more than would result from the exercise of revealed preferences.

I have no intention of contesting the necessity of utilizing revealed preferences as data at the physical or positive stage of the social sciences. But the awareness toward which Mr. Aron is leading us indicates that we cannot neglect a higher metaphysical or normative stage of the social sciences. It is at this stage that the conditions of the "good life" are posed, and from these conditions emerge the "reasonable preferences" which we have to compare to the "revealed preferences." Since none of us is an expert, there is no question of tyrannically imposing "reasonable preferences" on the "revealed preferences," but merely ascertaining how the latter can be made to approximate the former. If the intellectual were not bound to work for what is reasonable, and toward its acceptance, to what then should he devote himself?

VOEGELIN: I would like to raise one problem as briefly as possible, the one I consider most essential, namely, the organization of a "good society" for the "good life." This is an extremely delicate matter, a very difficult speculation for many reasons, which I shall try to explain. The difficulty lies in the fact that today there is no common accord as to what constitutes a good society and a good life, and the classic definitions are such that they would not be readily accepted today. Still, it will be necessary for me to go back to these classic definitions and use them at least as a point of departure, because they offer important insights into the meaning of the terms "good society" and "good life."

What I liked most about Mr. Aron's paper was his insistence on the fact that for a society to be well ruled from any standpoint, it must defer to the process of reasonable debate. One might say that this is the cornerstone of Western belief in constitutional government—government through reason. What then are the conditions for reasonable debate?

I would like to begin with a remark Einstein made about physics. One day Einstein remarked that the only unintelligible thing in the universe is its intelligibility. This admirably describes the problems of physics and the natural sciences in general, but especially physics. In the social sciences, and more especially in political science, we find ourselves in a much less favorable situation. We might say that there are many unintelligible things and that the only one which is not unintelligible is intelligibility. Here we find ourselves involved with a number of mysteries, which we must recognize as such, because we falsify the structure of reality as soon as we attempt to pierce the mystery by scientific means.

First let us see how the question of a "science of society" came about. We sometimes tend to forget this, and it is important to recall since it will immediately enable us to define the limits of what we can or cannot do through political science and political philosophy. The idea of a social science, of a political science in the classic sense, originated with medicine. The term *eidos*—ideas—originally signified the syndrome or set of symptoms used to identify an illness. This medical term subsequently passed over from Hippocratic medicine to the analysis of society, and in *The Peloponnesian War,* where the syndrome of *kinesis* was outlined, Thucydides uses the terms *eidos* and "idea" to describe the complex of symptoms characteristic of a social illness. It was only following this transfer of terms that Plato was able to ask himself whether it would be possible to conceive of a syndrome, or series of symptoms, for a healthy society. Thus any approach to political science is psychologically or emotionally colored by the realization of the evil in society and the desire to transform an unhealthy condition into a more healthy one. But this is more easily said than done. We are all sensitive to all sorts of ills in our society, for which we each doubtless have our own drastic remedies. But then we find ourselves stumbling, so to speak, from one unsatisfactory state to another, from one unhealthy society to another which may be even more unhealthy, unless we can actually claim that for one reason or another the newly created situation will be a definite improvement over the present. It is at this point that the following question arises: Do there exist objective criteria which enable us to define what is "better"? This is where we get into certain problems of actual political science and what I refer to as the "life of reason," which is nothing more than a fairly free translation of what Aristotle would have called *bios theoretikos.*

How can we arrive at objective opinions? First of all, distinctions have been made which ought to be used nowadays, but unfortunately they have gotten lost in the course of our daily lives. When Plato tried to compare what he considered objective truth with the prevailing opinions of what was good and bad in society, that is, the *doxa,* he introduced the term *philosophos* for the person who was striving to achieve this objective truth, and *episteme,* or science, for his knowledge. And he used the word "philosopher"—a term which has survived—as the antithesis of the *philodox* or amateur of prevailing opinions. The latter term has been forgotten. But a number of the difficulties we run into in intellectual discussions today stems from the fact that we use the word "philosophies" in precisely the opposite sense that Plato intended it, that is, we apply it to the *doxai* and use the word "philosopher" where Plato would have used *philodox.* Thus it is impossible today even to define or clarify the nature of the illness, because the illness itself has assumed the name of health.

At the risk of incurring the displeasure of certain people, I submit that what Plato called *philodox* we generally term "intellectual." Personally, I would be very upset if anyone classified me as an intellectual. I am opposed to the intellectual in the sense of *philodox,* that is, I am against the expression of an opinion which is not justified by rational analysis.

This brings us back to the question of where does rational analysis begin. I use the term "analysis" because Plato used it. By analysis I mean that we approach any study of society from the standpoint of the opinions of those around us. We find in our immediate circle both the opinions and the terminology expressing ideas of right or wrong; our job is to find the path leading from this vocabulary and these customs toward the objective element. This is introduced by the postulate that there is such a thing as human nature, and if we can discover what it consists of we can offer advice as to how society ought to be organized, since the organization of society should aim at the full flowering of human nature. However, there is no sense talking about good or bad institutions or making concrete suggestions about this or that social problem unless we first know what purpose or end these institutions are supposed to serve. This we cannot know unless we are familiar with the human nature which is going to develop within this social context. Thus the focal point of political science should always be what today we call philosophical anthropology, which in fact corresponds to the first chapter of *The Nicomachean Ethics*.

I shall concentrate on one basic point to which too little attention is currently paid. Plato and Aristotle suggested that human nature develops fully if it actualizes the participation in the transcendent being. Man is a creature who participates in the transcendent Nous and the transcendent Logos. Man leads a life of reason insofar as he cultivates this participation. Otherwise, if he begins to express ideas without cultivating this participation in the transcendent Logos, his conception of the human order will be twisted, for the over-all order of the individual is formed by his relation with the transcendent being. If this is eliminated, the result will be a warped idea of man's position in the universe. Then all the opinions expressed by those who maintain that man need not concern himself with the participation in transcendental reality—that is, the "immanentists" or "secularists," to employ contemporary terms—fall into the category of *doxa* or "opinion" in the technical sense of the term. So the "immanentists" or "secularists" are actually the disorganized spirits who are quite incapable of conceiving of ideas about the just order of society.

All this may seem somewhat aggressive, but let us now come to the facts of the matter. If we fail to adopt this attitude, the consequences will be unpleasant because the rational arguments concerning man's action and the order of society are based on certain premises which are closely connected with the attitude

I have just described. The first problem I want to stress is the problem of action. It is easy enough for us to talk of action— of rational action in that we co-ordinate the means with a view toward the end without wondering whether the end is particularly rational or reasonable, as Mr. de Jouvenel would call it. But we cannot settle for this if we want to speak objectively about problems of action. As long as we live in a group or society or within a larger cultural complex where there are accepted canons of action, there will be no problem, since we do not have to ask ourselves whether or not they are really rational. All we have to do is co-ordinate the means with the premises that tradition supplies us. But where tradition is questioned, or when we live in a pluralistic society of many varying opinions, we must have criteria in order to distinguish between opinions that are valid and those that are not. This means we can have no science of action, or no rational discussion or debate, as long as we have failed to agree rationally as to the ultimate goal, or, to hark back to the classical expression, the *summum bonum*. This is a matter of analysis. It does not follow that we can rationally determine the "sovereign good." Many people will say that perhaps it cannot be determined by rational means. But we must accept the consequences of these words, for if we subscribe to this thesis, then we may as well stop our discussions right now, for our debates will no longer have any rational basis.

The second point is that the *summum bonum* is not unrelated to the actualization of human nature. Here again we have the problem of transcendence, for the full flowering of human nature on the highest level is itself the search for transcendence. In classical antiquity, human nature was defined by man's openness to the transcendent being, or, to use a Bergsonian term, by the openness of the soul to transcendence. Thus this "openness of the soul," as a historical phenomenon which is the basis for all rational debate, is a postulate that we ought to take as our point of departure. If we do, however, we find ourselves faced with another problem concerning human nature. We all talk about human nature as though it were a concept descended from heaven. But we should remember that human nature is something the classical philosophers defined, and when we do not use it in the technical sense it is meaningless. This is why we ought to realize that certain uses of the term "human nature" are actually misuses. Nowadays we all talk about changing human nature, saying that by revolutions and reorganizing society we can effect such a change. This is patently impossible, because human nature in the classical sense, by its technical definition, is what cannot be changed, what remains constant.

Human nature is therefore a multiple problem: on the one hand it leads us to the question of transcendence and involvement in this transcendence, and on the other it is a term which has to be accepted in its classical sense, failing which it becomes meaningless. But when it is taken in its classical sense, the greatest part of contemporary ideological politics crumbles as material for debate, since we cannot discuss changes in human nature, which is the basis of Comtian positivism or any kind of Marxism: their whole credo is founded on the conviction that human nature *can* be changed, or in some way transfigured.

Everything I have just said was largely hypothetical, but I would like to emphasize that I personally agree with the classical position and would thus contend that a good society (in the classical sense, but also as the expression was used by John Stuart Mill in 1859) is one in which there is room for a life of reason to develop and flourish in such a way that men can devote themselves to it without embarrassment and make it an effective part of social organization. Such would be the definition of a good society. Where these conditions are lacking, serious spiritual troubles will develop. Then this problem: if our era is marked by such spiritual troubles, where do we have to begin in order to restore something resembling a good society? Here I should like to mention the positive aspect of the situation. To my mind, this is an aspect which has been sadly neglected, because the discussion has always turned around questions of ideology, but never around what is important for a good society.

It is striking that the places where we note a renaissance of the life of reason in our society, that is, a renewed awareness that participation in transcendence is central to the life of man and society, are in the sciences (and this does not mean the social sciences), whose very goal embodies an element which is healthy. The very fact of working at something healthy draws the attention of the researcher to the problems of rational order. This is why I find myself in the following curious situation when I try to orient myself and learn something: I discover I have very little to learn from the specialists in political science, who for the most part are not concerned about problems which relate to the order of the good society. Where I do find this concern is with the classical philologists, the specialists in mythology, the orientalists, and especially among theologians and philosophers who work closely with the various religions. Here you discover the foundations for reconstructing a Science of Order.

This brings us to the curious situation mentioned in Mr. Aron's paper. A unilateral debate is constantly emanating from these enclaves of the life of reason which still do exist in our society, and at the present time are perhaps even increasing. Here rational discussion does go on and a compact body of science concerning the ideologies, for instance, is being compiled. But there is no dialogue, for those for whom the discussion is intended, the ideologists, refuse to participate; they simply ignore the works in question. A kind of iron curtain exists not between East and West, but within the West itself, between what might be called the "con-substantial" Western society, which is still living the life of reason and perhaps even advancing within it, and those who turn their backs on it.

In order to present clearly all sides of the problem, I shall have to list the various ways and techniques used to keep the life of reason from making its unpleasant presence felt. As a matter of fact, we have developed a whole range of techniques to prevent discussion: the use of long speeches in place of rational give-and-take, in keeping with the tactics used by Protagoras in the Platonic dialogue of the same name; the "valet" psychology, which consists of trying to figure out the opponent's motives instead of engaging him in rational discussion; classification, which means pinning a label on him, etc. Beside these evasive tactics which aim at skirting the problem, we should also mention the systematic techniques which have been elaborated into whole systems whose goal is to stifle any discussion. For example, positivism and logical empiricism are based on the premise that from the standpoint of methodology only those methods analogous to the methods of the physical sciences can produce valid results in the field of the social sciences. Anyone who resorts to this argument automatically precludes any possibility of discussion about anything relating to political science in the classical sense of the term.

One specifically German invention which unfortunately, like so many other German inventions such as Marxism, seems to have spread throughout the world is the theory of *Wertbeziehung* and the idea that in science it is possible to constitute an object by relating the subject or question to a set of values, preferably contemporary values. If you introduce the notion of values as the point of reference for the choice of objects to be studied, you have simultaneously stifled any discussion of these values, since the question is limited to ascertaining what the controlling categories are for the selection of the objects. Whenever anyone refers to values and says that they lie beyond the pale of rational discussion and must be accepted as contemporary values without resubmitting them to further debate, it becomes obvious that the whole system of the *Wertbeziehende Methode,* as the Germans call it, is merely another instrument for preventing discussion.

I could list a number of other similar techniques, and if you add them all up you will doubtless see that a large portion of what currently passes as rational discussion in political science and the social sciences is not that at all; it is pure ideological rhetoric. This situation should be of major interest to all of us, and I submit that a renaissance of the life of reason, consonant with its original definition, is one of the most urgent tasks that lies before us.

ARON: The doctrine we have just heard presented with such uncompromising rationality can be résuméed as follows: for there to be any rational or reasonable discussion of politics, there first has to be agreement on the common good. There can be no agreement on the supreme good, however, if one does not have a conception of human nature. This conception implies the immutability of human nature, however, and this is linked to a certain conception of man's participation in a transcendent reality, a transcendent Nous. I believe that Professor Voegelin himself would admit that in a given cultural system, such as that of the United States, the possibility for rational discussion does exist, even if there is no conscious awareness of the supreme good. But he would perhaps add that the only reason this rational discussion is possible under the American system is because in a sense this system is the translation of a philosophy of the supreme good and of human nature. This "translation" is debased because the superior concepts have tended to be lost. Yet it is their invisible presence which enables rational dialogue to persist and go on. Professor Voegelin has already reminded us how difficult it is to discuss a thesis of this sort. If one rejects his premises and postulates, rational discussion is obviously circumscribed, since the most one can do is pursue the discussion to the point of irreconcilable values. This means at best a partial discussion, which will break down when one reaches the point of supreme values. This first hypothesis is the one which proved true in the course of the present conference, and this is the type of discussion for which someone Professor Voegelin knows as well as I, and perhaps even better, provided the model: Max Weber. Weber accepted the possibility of rational discussion as to the means, the institutions, and the organizations, but he said that this discussion ended and came to grief when it came to fundamental affirmations of values. Rational dialogue, he claimed, stopped at this point.

But the other hypothesis, whereby one accepts the supreme good and human nature, poses at least two difficulties. First, we have to know how far reason is capable of determining the transcendent Nous in which the minds of men participate. Second, even if we accept the immutability of human nature—and to my mind this is self-evident; if we talk of human nature, it means it does not change, it is a question of definition—then on what level of abstraction does what we call human nature reveal itself, and to what extent can this conception of human nature comprise a kind of finality and not be defined simply by what psychoanalysts would call a system of impulsions.

Thus we see that no matter which of the two terms we choose, the problems remain impressive.

ANDRZEJEWSKI: Is the idea that human nature can change really such a mad one? Personally, I do not believe it is all that absurd. We already have sufficient knowledge of biology to know that the species is not fixed, that selection does operate on the human level, and that certain types do disappear while others multiply more rapidly. If we move toward the possibility of a planned, manipulated selection, we could probably change human nature fairly rapidly. Moreover, there is the imminent possibility that we will find a way to manipulate the genes. If all this helps increase man's average intelligence or lower the level of his aggressive tendencies, the impact on future societies will obviously be tremendous.

VOEGELIN: We must realize that the idea of man is not given to us automatically by history, but emerges gradually. That men are truly men and that all men are equal represents a considerable advance, which is imputable to Western philosophy beginning with the fifth century B.C. The idea of human equality became clear only in the light of man's equality before God. The idea of man grew up through the experience of the universal existence of men equal before a universal God, and no problem of biology can alter this concept. When you introduce the problem of perfectibility, you move to another plane. On the one hand we have history, during which man has realized his possibilities in a most remarkable way: think of his domination of nature, for example. But this has not altered nature, which remains immutably consistent with the classical definition. But the idea of perfectibility in the ideological sense, the "transfiguration" à la Condorcet into a progressive or communist superhuman, into Nietzsche's Dionysian or Comte's positivist superman, poses a totally different problem. Rational argumentation can show you that a specific type of perfectibility is the equivalent of metastasis or transfiguration and that here we come in conflict with what we know empirically about human nature.

IYER: The question of perfectibility or nonperfectibility cannot be resolved through experience. This is true not only because the facts and values are intermixed, but also because this question implies a whole cosmology. If you really want to start a debate on the subject of human nature, its possibilities of change and perfection, you must answer the question: "What is your cosmology?" In fact it is significant that Plato, Rousseau, and Gandhi, as opposed to Marx and numerous other political theorists, all had a theory of education. Is it really possible to speak of changes in human nature without proposing some theory of education?

VOEGELIN: I would like to re-emphasize that what I presented was not a personal opinion, but more or less a rundown of historical facts. Reason and its works were discovered at a certain period in history. The attendant concepts such as human nature, human rights, freedom, etc., are symbolic extrapolations, if I may call them that, of certain experiences which I called transcendent. I doubt that the terms we use every day in our discussions have other roots than these experiences. For this reason, it is impossible to analyze the structure of society without referring to the operations of the life of reason. We did not really go into detail about social structures in the spiritual or intellectual sense of the term, but if, for instance, you want to know in which direction Chinese civilization is evolving or what its affinities and differences with communism are, you cannot reply without studying the history of China and the spiritual edifice of Chinese civilization. If you pose a similar question about India and Indian civilization, the same will hold true. And this cannot be accomplished by the methods of logical positivism or empiricism, which deny that there is a problem of the life of reason.

What is more, there are political overtones to what I suggest. By concentrating on the problems of the industrial society, we have perhaps tended to forget that we live not only in the age of industrial society but also in the era of ideological movements, ideological regimes, and ideological wars, and that in our time tens of millions of people have died to further these ideologies. This is a fundamental fact. And I shall add here that to insist on the problems of the life of reason is equivalent to a sort of new declaration of Human Rights *against* the ideologies. I often say to my students: "God did not create this world for the ideologists alone; man also has the right to live here." What then is man? Here is a problem for the life of reason.

To come back to our discussion, obviously it is possible to carry on an important discussion within the framework of a given set of cultural traditions and general premises, about which there is common accord. This is what we have done here. It can be done with complete rationality, without questioning any of the premises, because they are far enough removed not to interfere with the concrete problems under review. For all practical purposes, this level of concrete discussion probably suffices for international exchanges, unless we run afoul of an ideology with universal pretentions. Then, of course, we have to move to another kind of discussion. But our level suffices for most of our purposes. It is in this sense that I would qualify our discussions as most enlightening and fruitful.

TALMON: In the course of our discussions we have not dealt with the problem of nationalism, which to me seems of major importance when we consider the present world situation. We discussed the industrial society and tried to juxtapose three blocs by comparing their respective effects on the industrial system and the effects of this system on each of them. But may I remind our friends that for the past hundred or hundred and fifty years there were thinkers who already believed in the industrial society. Industry was considered an important factor of peace and unification. The second half of the nineteenth century and the first half of the twentieth have shown that the most important of all these factors was nationalism. Consequently, its absence in our debates seemed to me a regrettable omission.

Nothing is more indefinite than nationalism. It has degenerated into Fascism; it can also become a factor of spiritual freedom, as has been proved in our time. And, as one listener suggested, we have no idea into what it may develop in Russia. We can hope that communism may become a sort of national religion, guiding the Soviets as an exigency in which it would be extremely difficult to distinguish (as has sometimes been the case for France) nationalistic pride from ideological proselytism.

Finally, it was my impression that the over-all tone of our discussions was optimistic. I was struck by Mr. Kennan's remark that *1984* would be inconceivable in Russia. And in his paper Mr. Aron quickly dismissed the Fascist movements by observing: "These credos are no longer respectable; in modern societies they are impossible." It appears that the specter of Fascism during the past few years does not frighten or concern us in the least, and this surprises and disturbs me.

CONCLUSION

ARON: I thought that the least unsatisfactory way to conclude our discussions would be for me to go back and refer to the main questions that I had raised at the start and try to determine to what extent we have answered them, or whether we have even dealt with them at all. For if certain of the questions which seemed important to us were not dealt with, we may be able to read as much meaning into our silence or refusal to reply as we can glean from the answers we gave the other questions.

First of all, I would like to answer Professor Talmon and comment on a remark made by Mr. Sartori.

Actually, both Mr. Sartori and Mr. Talmon have reproached me for having been overly optimistic both in my report and in these discussions. Mr. Talmon reminded me of something which made a deep impression on me—the fact that a few years ago a discussion such as this would have taken place in an obsessive atmosphere dominated by the specter of Nazism and Fascism, whereas here these subjects hardly entered the discussion. I was quite taken by this observation, because I found it to be profoundly true. I do not believe I have committed an intellectual error; I did not say that movements such as Nazism or Fascism might not arise again some time in the future. But undeniably I was wrong to act as though I had forgotten them. We have no right to forget what happened during the past twenty years by simply asserting that today the situation has improved. So I am tempted to plead guilty, merely adding that, in spite of my reputation, I am in a certain sense an irrepressible optimist. I cannot help believing that in the long run an evolution in the direction of reason is more probable than an evolution toward madness and catastrophe. When I think about it, I see no reasonable reason to believe in my own optimism. When people reproach me for it, I am immediately tempted to say: "How right you are." But perhaps for reasons of temperament or background, in the end I always revert to a certain optimistic outlook and say: "Now look, when we have the means to produce goods in such quantities that neither exploitation nor extreme inequality is necessary, it seems unreasonable to believe that the classes will continue to fight as they did in the time when there was a fixed volume of wealth to be shared and it was impossible to give a great deal to some without taking a great deal away from the others." I know that people may still go on fighting over inessentials, or when there is no reason to fight, because man is as he is. But I inevitably tend to suspect that reason will prevail in the long run. I know I am wrong. So I can only explain the overly optimistic tone which dominated our discussions by what certain scientists call "the personal equation."

The first question which was posed by my paper was contained in the title "The Concept of Industrial Society." It is interesting to note that we remain divided into two schools of thought, two attitudes vis-à-vis this notion of industrial society. One accepts or does not accept the notion for methodological reasons, or for reasons of basic disagreement. The methodological objection is the following: The separation of the rational elements of economic organization, in relation to the whole of the social context, presupposes a method of generalization that I find legitimate but that others may not. In order to understand that we have not reached an agreement, I will venture to say that it was a matter of two well-defended positions. One of the most serious problems of methodology in the social sciences is determining to what extent the conceptualization of industrial society is a valid technique. But the problem is not only one of methodology; it is also one of essence. For although I stated the concept as a question, it suggests a certain community of societies which accepts the same sort of economic organization, and consequently implies a tendency on the part of various societies to resemble each other more and more. This, of course, is very much open to debate. To the end of our discussions, there were some who preferred to keep the whole notion of industrial society between quotation marks, or who put the adjective "Aronian" after it—which was quite flattering to me. By this they simply meant they were using the term because I had used it, but that they did not agree with it. This discussion could not be resolved because it stems from certain basic diffi- culties in the methods of the social sciences, as well as a differ- ence of opinion in the interpretation of history.

Nevertheless, we all did accept the fact that there are certain salient features of economic and technical organization which cannot help but be transmitted throughout the world. Thus it is easy enough to see where we do agree as well as where we differ.

Next, there was a question we did not discuss, because we all more or less shared the same opinion about it: this was the tend- ency of ideological conflicts to abate in Western societies. It is somewhat odd that I devoted several pages in my report to this "devaluation" of the nineteenth-century ideological conflicts; several speakers alluded to it, including Mr. Kennan, but as if to say: "Yes, we all agree; no need to discuss it any further." Perhaps because we did not have a militant socialist here, no one contested the fact that the quarrels over the status of prop- erty, or the means of regulating the economy are still today the principal source of conflict, as they were twenty-five or fifty years ago. The absence of discussion about the historical fact that, relatively speaking, there has been an abatement of ideo- logical conflicts indicates to me that we all basically agreed on this as well. If anyone had objected seriously to it we would have discussed it more. Thus we accepted the fact that today the problems of private property vs. public property, market mechanisms, or planning are relative and complementary rather than absolute concepts, and that, in the realm of ideals, reality always comes up with a variation of these ideal types.

The third problem I had raised was that of the basic difference, or lack of difference, between the Soviet and Western societies.

We have talked a great deal about this, and all we can say is that we neither completely agreed nor were we in violent opposition. The dominant tone of our discussion of the subject, from beginning to end, was one of questioning. We more or less consented to the fact that in Soviet business there is a rationalization of production methods which is inevitable and which tends to make the internal structure of Soviet industry ever closer to that of American or European industry. We also thought, almost without exception, that if we consider the organization of the economy as a whole, we see an evolution toward rationalization—in the sense of increasing pragmatism and less and less ideological obsession—as a distinct possibility. As the Soviet economy grows more complex and more productive, the taboos, the ideological imperatives such as "25 per cent for investments" or "collectivism in agriculture" have a tendency to weaken and give way to a more opportunistic, more pragmatic, and more reasonable attitude, in the sense that the West employs the term "reasonable."

But thereafter it was difficult to conclude categorically either that these two types of societies were growing closer together or moving further apart. It was difficult because there still remain in Soviet society today many elements which are very different from our society and which do not tend to disappear, and also because, as one spectator pointed out, at every stage in the growth of an industrial society, new alternatives arise. Thus it is possible that the differences of the early stages may disappear, but that others may arise in later stages.

If I had to sum up the basic reasons for our uncertainty, I would say that it was first of all because the idea of the millennium was so closely associated with the birth and evolution of

Soviet society that it seems to me premature to state that Soviet society—or at least its leaders—is now going to accept the fact of merely being what it is and give up the idea of becoming the only absolutely valid society or of building an earthly paradise. Millenarianism is still a sufficient force in Soviet society so that we cannot categorically state that a society of this type will tend to become increasingly reasonable. I might add that this idea of the millennium is all the more difficult to eradicate because, in a certain way, it is the basis of the Soviet state itself.

What has always struck me in the few conversations I have had with people from the Soviet Union is the fact that they find it extremely hard to admit that Soviet society is governed by the Party, that is, by a few men and not by the proletariat. "It is the proletariat which rules because Khrushchev is in power" is the type of equation which is the cornerstone of Soviet political society itself, and it is terribly difficult for them to give it up without consenting to an almost revolutionary transformation.

The second reason is that there is a sort of one-party logic from which Soviet society cannot easily free itself. What I call the "logic" of the single party is the refusal to hold free elections, to allow the formation of other political groups, or to permit a certain amount of unfettered intellectual discussion. In a society which claims to be harmonious and to be ruled by the masses, it is difficult to accept the freedom of discussion which presupposes that a society be heterogeneous. It is quite possible, if the Soviet Union is lucky enough to have a succession of top political leaders who are reasonable and paternal—benevolent despots—that their society will evolve in the direction we desire. But so long as they have a one-party system we cannot exclude the possibility that from the internal struggle among vying factions there may one day emerge a despot who is *not* benevolent. I believe that even Mr. Kennan, who is the most optimistic of us all, would not be as dogmatic as, say, Isaac Deutscher, who claims that in terms of the Soviet society we can predict what kind of leader it will have. I must add, however, that in applying this theory he came to the conclusion that Khrushchev could not become the top Soviet leader, and this would seem to cast some doubt on how close the connection is between Soviet society and the personal characteristics of its premier.

I think that there is a third reason for our lack of certainty: In any social context, industrial society is only a means or an instrument, and nothing proves that the Soviet leaders aspire to have Soviet citizens live the same way Western leaders would like their citizens to live. The nature of the means of what we call "industrial society" in no sense permits us to conclude from the increasing resemblance between economic organizations that the societies themselves—the ideologies, or, finally, the philosophies or ways of life—will also come to resemble each other.

The fourth question I raised was that of the *tiers monde*— the "third world"—and we did talk about this, but not at great length, because the question as I stated it was: "Do the non-Western countries have to follow the same path? What facets of Western society do they want to, must they, *can* they imitate? Today, to what extent does the West want to transmit its political institutions?" My impression is that we were all somewhat embarrassed by this discussion, for easily understandable reasons. First of all, we are not smug enough about our political institutions to be wholly desirous of transmitting them, and we are too conscious of the reproaches made to us concerning our imperialism or ideological imperialism to be in the least tempted to say today to the peoples of Africa or Asia: "Adopt a parliamentary-style democracy, such as the British, the American, or even—if you really want to—the French." No one here inclines toward this sort of ambition or imperialism. And yet, insofar as we do hold to these institutions, it is likewise impossible for us to say to our friends in Asia and Africa: "This system is fine for us, but not for you." If we do, we shall rightly be accused of racism, of considering that institutions valid for us are not valid for them. We thus find ourselves constantly caught between the Charybdis of ideological imperialism and the Scylla of racism, and no matter in what direction we move we are immediately attacked. In order to get around this prob-

lem—for after all man is an ingenious creature—we have discovered a method which consists of making a distinction between
the concrete political institutions—parties, elections, parliament,
which we recognize as having a specific place in history—and
the ideas which inspire them—liberalism, free discussion, respect
for the will of the governed by those who govern, which seem
to us to be universally valid. Mr. Kennan made this distinction,
as did Mr. Asoka Mehta. I believe that it is a very basic one,
but it is rather a point of departure than a conclusion, for the
following reason: It seems to me that the spread of the industrial
society is bound to have a fairly obvious political repercussion
—the weakening of traditional regimes. Industrial society trans-
forms basically the sense of time and tradition. It is impossible,
at a time when society itself is being revolutionized in order to
adapt itself to a scientific method of production, for a power
to be founded solely on the fact of its previous existence. The
traditional basis of power—except in rare cases when it was
based upon reason—may lie in some religious value or tradition.
I submit that these two kinds of traditional bases of political
power are presently crumbling throughout the world, precisely
because of the impact upon them of the industrial society. This
being the case, it is not such an easy job to avoid the choice
between the system of free discussion on a political basis and
the system of a single party which, in the name of an absolute
ideological truth, claims to mold society in its own image. This
is not to say that there are not certain intermediate solutions;
both Western societies and non-Western societies have found
intermediate formulas. In France, we have recently found a
formula which might be called a consular republic, or the res-
toration of a constitutional, nonhereditary monarchy. This is
an intermediary formula which utilizes certain elements of past
political regimes to escape the alternative of a multiparty system which is ineffective and a one-party system that is not
wanted. There are a number of intermediary political forms,
but they are difficult to define and do not function well over
a long period of time. I do not want to say that the choice be-

tween a one-party and a multiparty system is the basic choice for all mankind, but I nevertheless do believe that they mark the two inevitable directions of political regimes in a civilization which witnesses the disappearance of traditional bases for power, leaving only individuals, their ambitions and desires. In this situation, either a group of men girds itself with an ideology and imposes it on everyone else, or free discussion is allowed; but if free discussion is to result in vested authority, there has to be a minimum of agreement on the essentials. We were extremely hesitant to venture any further than the area of generalities, because the situation is extremely difficult, and perhaps we more or less felt what I have just tried to express.

The fifth and final question which was raised by my paper is the one we discussed at most length, and I note this with a great deal of satisfaction because it was the question I was most concerned with, the one I thought most important, and the one which, at bottom, is the justification of the entire seminar.

This question was: Industrial society is not an end; it is a certain type of social organization which provides the means to combat efficiently poverty and impotence. It is normal that all societies aspire to adopt these means to power and wealth, because we cannot survive without them. And yet, however important may be the economic and sociological discussions concerning the stages of growth, the methods of growth, the combination of the control of the population and the development of the resources—all these sociological-economic problems which we discuss in our courses, our books, and sometimes in our dreams—the real question which confronts the West is *knowing what it is and what it wants,* aside from vast factories and a rise in the standard of living.

On this point, I had one or two thoughts I would like to pass on to you. The first is that everyone, or almost everyone here— whatever our education and background in the fields of sociology, economics, philosophy, history, natural sciences—was interested in this problem. In other words, I believe that in the West we have reached a stage of philosophical and religious reflection, not directed against the successes of the positive scientists, but in fact, in *terms* of their success, for it has led us back to the fundamental issues. These are: What meaning are we to give life? What is the "good life"? What is the good society? In other words, it is because of the success of the positive methods that we have become aware of the limitations they imply and of the necessity of raising fundamental questions, ultimate questions. This said, there is no denying the fact that the discussions we have had throughout this week have been difficult—it could hardly be otherwise—because in a way we were all asking the same ultimate questions, but the criteria and the methods used differed widely. In my paper I noted at the very outset this absence of philosophical unity. I think that on the whole the evolution of the seminar confirmed that the problem of discussion was a difficult one. But though it was difficult it was not impossible, since most of us recognized simultaneously that we were asking the same questions and trying to answer them by different means and with different words.

On one level, the discussions took the form of a critical review of society and mass culture, and a reminder of the precautions that have to be taken to prevent the evolution of this society from ruining men's lives and eliminating the contact between man and nature. Second, in many of the papers there was an obvious yearning for what I shall vaguely call "something religious." Several of the speakers felt that the great question men would have to discuss and deal with, whenever they had solved their material problems, would be the meaning of human existence; at the same time they thought that religion—whether or not it assumed one of its several dogmatic forms—would be an increasingly important problem of future history, one which would occupy each of us more and more.

Professor Oppenheimer led our discussions in a third direction by pondering the multiplicity of intellectual worlds and the quest for unity. The arts and sciences have become so specialized and separated from each other that no one is any longer capable of embracing the whole world of culture. This we know. But for the very reason that a complete unity of the world of culture is out of the question, it is essential that our words, addressed to the world at large, contain the maximum of essential truths uncovered by the various sciences. We all realized the extraordinary difficulty of the problems, but I believe that we were also aware that we were not debating a problem raised arbitrarily in terms of a conference, but a serious and real problem which affects the very life of the culture at a time when the accumulation of knowledge and the subtlety of specific methods no longer permits any single mind, however ubiquitous, to embrace the whole.

Another area of discussion was that of the social scientists, who talked in terms of political or social sciences. These speakers hoped to see the ultimate questions—and I might almost say the answers to the ultimate questions—emerge from social practice itself. I think that many sociologists would tell us that it is impossible to codify into a system our replies to the ultimate questions because each one of us states what he is and what he wants; what we can do, though, is discover from the lives of various individuals what they really want as ultimate values. It is impossible to list the replies, but the essence of them is contained in social practice itself, as the sciences of society understand it.

Finally, Professor Voegelin made a very careful distinction between the ideologies which imprison the majority of men—and perhaps, if he had been less polite, he might have said the majority of those participating in this seminar—and the truths of reason that philosophy is capable of grasping.

I presented this attitude in a humanistic form, and I apologize for it, but I do not in the least think that Professor Voegelin was wrong, for the necessary condition for a philosophical discussion is not to be ideologists, not men of opinion or *doxa,* to borrow a word from Plato. If we are merely men of *doxa,* all we can do is contradict each other's views, and reasonable discussion becomes impossible. Perhaps, however, he exaggerated the situation slightly, in that a considerable amount of reasonable discussion is possible if we presuppose common values or common desires. Within societies, even though there may not be a rational awareness of the supreme good, there is nonetheless an obscure or imperfect awareness of it. Thanks to this fact and to human nature, there can be reasonable discussions, even among people who resort to dogmatism. Those who claim to deny reason are not as bad as they think they are. They, too, in a way believe in some kind of reason, even though they may state that only opinions and ideologies matter.

I believe that this sums up fairly well the essence of our discussions, including the answers we gave or those we were hesitant to give, the questions we shelved and those we concentrated on. I think that the two essential points might well be the following: Is there a fundamental difference between Soviet society and Western society? It would be rash, and probably erroneous, to assert it. Is a reconciliation likely in the near future between these two types of social organization? It would be almost as dangerous to believe this. In all probability, the exchanges—which we trust will be nonviolent—between the Soviet and Western societies will continue over a relatively long period, but it is possible that, realizing the absurdity of war, this exchange may become more and more a real dialogue and not, as it has been so often in the past, a double monologue. The problem is not that both societies should be identical, but rather that they should mutually recognize the right of the other to exist and discover the points on which a difference actually exists between them.

I shall sum up the second basic point in the following manner: the awareness of the need for and the difficulty of having a philosophical discussion within the West itself. I believe that we are all convinced of the need for this exchange, and we also know how difficult it is, not simply because science so impresses the layman, but also because in the past there was generally an accepted method of philosophical reflection. Today there is no such unanimously accepted method of philosophical reflection; there are several methods, and even when professional philosophers meet they are not always able to come to an agreement any more easily than we were able to here.

A LIST OF THE PARTICIPANTS

S. ANDRZEJEWSKI, a sociologist who teaches in England at the Brunel College of Technology.

RAYMOND ARON, professor at the Sorbonne in Paris, a philosopher, economist, and author who presided over the discussions. His numerous works, from his *Introduction to the Theory of History* to his recent studies on the industrial society, have been translated into several languages.

RUDOLF BICANIC, an economist, sociologist, and professor at the University of Zagreb.

GEORGE E. G. CATLIN, known for his work in political science; New College, Oxford.

LUIS DIEZ DEL CORRAL, professor at the University of Madrid, author of *The Rape of Europe*.

JEANNE HERSCH, professor of philosophy at the University of Geneva, author of works of philosophy and political thought.

RAGHAVAN IYER, Fellow of St. Antony's College, Oxford.

BERTRAND DE JOUVENEL, author and economist who has written works on political theory; Paris.

GEORGE KENNAN, former chairman of the Policy Planning Council of the United States State Department, former U.S. Ambassador to Moscow, and a member of the Institute for Advanced Study, Princeton.

CHARLES LINDBLOM, professor of political economy at Yale University.

ASOKA MEHTA, vice-president of the Socialist group in the Indian Parliament and author of several works on the evolution of India.

CHARLES MORAZÉ, historian, professor at the *Institut d'Études Politiques,* Paris.

ROBERT OPPENHEIMER, nuclear physicist, director of the Institute for Advanced Study, Princeton.

MICHAEL POLANYI, scholar and philosopher, Fellow of Merton College, Oxford. His many works include his recent philosophical study, *Personal Knowledge.*

M. M. POSTAN, who teaches at Cambridge, is renowned for his work in the history of economics.

EUGENE V. ROSTOW, economist, professor of American history at Cambridge.

EDGAR SALIN, sociologist and author, professor at the University of Basel.

GIOVANNI SARTORI, professor of political science at the University of Florence.

MANÈS SPERBER, French sociologist, critic and novelist, author of *Le Talon d'Achille.*

J. L. TALMON, professor at the University of Jerusalem and author of the well-known work, *The Origins of Totalitarian Democracy.*

ERIC VOEGELIN, political theorist, professor at the University of Munich.